CHERRIES
&
MULBERRIES

To:
The Four Ms
(Mum, Magic and Jane's master tasters, Mat and Matilda)
with all our love

This edition published in 2018 in Great Britain and the USA by Prospect Books at 26 Parke Road, London, SW13 9NG

British Library Cataloguing in Publication Data:
A catalogue entry for this book is available from the British Library.

ISBN 13: 978-1-909248-56-4

Printed by the Gutenberg Press Ltd., Malta.

THE ENGLISH KITCHEN

CHERRIES & MULBERRIES

GROWING AND COOKING

JANE MCMORLAND HUNTER

AND

SALLY HUGHES

PROSPECT BOOKS

2018

TABLE OF CONTENTS

INTRODUCTION

Cherry Tree Lane and Mulberry Walk will lead you to a world
of wondrous fruits.

(With thanks to P. L. Travers and King James I)

Cherries and mulberries have much in common: they have
both been an important part of man's diet for thousands
of years, they grow on beautiful trees, and, perhaps most
importantly they are both fleeting visitors to our kitchens in summer.
They also have intriguing histories related to the world of art; in
the case of cherries, this is the story of the ornamental tree and the
traditional Japanese cherry blossom festivals which have now spread
and take place around the world; with mulberries it is the story of silk,
that delicate and highly sought-after product of the humble silkworm.

Wild cherries have grown in northern Europe and North America
since prehistoric times and sour cherries have been cultivated in
Britain ever since the Romans arrived. Cherry fairs, held annually
in summer, gave villagers an opportunity to make merry and
writers from Shakespeare to D. H. Lawrence have set romantic or
ribald scenes in cherry orchards. More demurely, A. E. Housman
commemorated the beauty of cherry blossom in verse.

Black mulberries originated in central Asia, travelling across Europe on the ancient trade routes, dropping their luscious fruits as they went. White mulberries came from China, where they were catalysts for the highly lucrative and closely guarded silk trade. Red mulberries are native to the United States and although they are famed for neither berries nor silk, they do grow into remarkably pretty trees.

They are both delicate fruits and do not travel well. It is often hard to get a perfectly ripe mulberry from the tree to one's mouth, let alone survive a journey by road, sea or rail. Cherries are easy to buy in season, but bought fruit is rarely at its best (having been picked slightly under-ripe to survive the rigours of transport) and you never see the interesting and unusual varieties for sale. In fact you rarely see any specific varieties for sale; they are all usually simply labelled 'sweet cherries'. Sour cherries are even harder to find. The solution is to grow your own.

For hundreds of years most cherries grew on tall, stately trees which looked wonderful in spring, with their clouds of blossom reaching up to the sky, but were a nightmare to pick, requiring long ladders and a good head for heights. Breeding advances in the late twentieth century mean that all cherries can now be successfully grown on little trees which will fit in almost any garden, or even in a container if you have no garden at all. Mulberries grow on trees which acquire the patina of age when still quite young, their gnarled and twisty branches giving them a shape which is beautiful all year round. They were reasonably sized trees already; however, in 2017, after years of breeding, a new strain of mulberry bush became available, meaning these berries can also be successfully grown in containers.

Both fruits are rich in antioxidants which help to protect against the effects of ageing and the stresses of modern life. This, along with mineral and vitamin advantages, means that you owe it to yourself to include more cherries and mulberries in your diet. The anti-inflammatory properties of cherries have been recognised for centuries and cherry juice is considered an effective treatment for joint conditions such as arthritis and gout. Mulberries are surprisingly

high in iron, with a small portion containing a quarter of your daily allowance. There you see, good for you as well as delicious.

In the kitchen, both fruits are endlessly adaptable, providing the basis for sweet and savoury dishes as well as preserves and drinks. We have included over fifty recipes here, ranging from a light refreshing cherry sangria to a winter braise of venison with cherry sauce, from smoked duck and cherry salad to a late summer pudding with mulberries, alongside a delicious array of cakes, biscuits, chocolates and strudels.

We make no apology for the fact that this is the second time we have included mulberries in a book. They made a brief appearance in our book *Berries: Growing and Cooking*, but there was not enough space there to do them justice. Their history, the story of silk, their beauty in the garden and their diversity in the dining room all meant that we wanted to write about them again. We hope that you agree with us.

THE STORY OF CHERRIES

A ripe cherry…so full of juice and tender of skin that it would burst at the very sight of a bushel basket.

(Edward Bunyard, *The Anatomy of Dessert*, 1933)

Wild cherries must have been one of the seasonal highlights for prehistoric man, with cherry stones found at Neolithic and Bronze Age (5,000-1,500 BC) sites in Turkey, Italy, Portugal and central Europe. They were quickly recognized as valuable trees as they provided food, timber and fuel. Given sufficient time and space, the trees will spread by means of suckers. In ancient Britain space was readily available and there were no intensive farmers demanding instant yields, so small copses of cherry trees slowly developed.

Wild sweet cherries growing in Asia Minor were cultivated by the Chinese 3,000 years ago and ancient records show that there were cherry orchards in Mesopotamia in the eighth century BC. Apparently the Assyrian King Sargon II cultivated them because he liked their fragrance. Herodotus, writing in the fifth century BC, describes a community living at the foot of the Ural Mountains:

They live on the fruit of a certain tree, the name of which is Ponticum; in size it is about equal to our fig tree, and it bears

a fruit like a bean, with a stone inside. When the fruit is ripe, they strain it through cloths; the juice which runs off is black and thick, and is called by the natives 'aschy'. They lap this up with their tongues, and also mix it with milk for a drink; while they make the lees, which are solid, into cakes, and eat them instead of meat; for they have but few sheep in their country, in which there is no good pasturage. Each of them dwells under a tree, and they cover the tree in winter with a cloth of thick white felt, but take off the covering in summer time. No one harms these people, for they are looked upon as sacred – they do not even possess any warlike weapons. When their neighbours fall out, they make up the quarrel; and when one flies to them for refuge, he is safe from all hurt. They are called the Argippaeans.

Nearly all modern cherries are descended from two wild forms: the sweet cherry (*Prunus avium*) and the sour cherry (*P. cerasus*). The names themselves give clues to this fruit's heritage. Most directly the word cherry comes from the Old French *cherise* and the Latin *cerasus* which, in turn, come from the Greek *kerasos* and the Accadian word *karsu* used by the Assyrians and Babylonians. Originally the Greek name was thought to have come from the city Kerasos in Asia Minor (now Giresun in Turkey), but it is far more likely that the city was called after the fruit, which passed through it on the way to distant markets.

The Roman general Lucullus is credited with introducing cultivated cherries to Western Europe, with Pliny the Elder stating in his *Natural History* that before 74 BC there were no cherry trees in Italy, presumably referring to cultivated plants. Lucullus successfully conquered the region of Pontus, but as well as being a great general he was also keen on his food and brought, among other things, cherry trees back to Italy, in all probability the very fruits described by Herodotus. According to Pliny: 'In the span of a hundred and twenty years they have crossed the ocean and spread as far as Britain.' Records confirm this, with cultivated cherries recorded in Britain

in 46 AD, just three years after the Roman invasion. By 79 AD the Romans had planted extensive cherry orchards, especially in Kent where they could easily be transported to the city of London.

After the Romans left Britain horticulture in general declined, only really continuing in monastery gardens. Specialized cherry orchards, called *cherruzerd* or *orto cersor*, did survive since the fruits were so popular. In *Piers Plowman* William Langland describes people enjoying baked apples and cherries, no doubt a pleasant change for the poor whose basic diet consisted of vegetables and little else. Seasonal fruit was often given as a gift; in Edmund Spenser's *Faerie Queene* Diana's maid is wooed with:

...pleasing gifts for her purvey'd
Queen apples and red cherries from the tree.

Records at the convent at Ely show that fruit sometimes had to be imported to satisfy demand. Fruit cultivation in Europe continued with new varieties being introduced, particularly in Flanders and France. In 1364 the two gardens belonging to Charles V of France, Tournelles and St Paul, contained 1,125 cherry trees compared to a mere 115 apple trees and 100 pear trees.

In the sixteenth century, cherry growing was revived in England. Cherries were attractive as well as productive trees and were often planted in the ornamental areas of gardens, lining the avenues along which the grand ladies took their walks. Henry VIII loved cherries, as did Elizabeth I, and both attempted to free England from her dependence on imports. So keen was he to impress his monarch that when Sir Francis Carew knew that Elizabeth I intended to visit him he covered an entire cherry tree with damp canvas to retard the fruits so they would be perfect for her.

In 1533 Richard Harris, Henry VIII's fruiterer, travelled to Europe in search of new and improved cultivars. He brought back cultivars from Flanders and France which were planted at a new orchard at Teynham in Kent. The orchard had apples, pears and other fruits as well as cherries and was a few miles west of the present National Fruit

Cherries & Mulberries

Collection at Brogdale. There are no records of the exact cultivars he brought back, but the orchard was believed to have been planted in a quincunx pattern, with four trees at the corners of a square and a single tree in the centre, which was both attractive and practical for the all-important pollination. For those who took the matter seriously, cherry growing could be a profitable enterprise. The Earl of Leicester planted a thirty-acre cherry orchard near Sittingbourne in Kent. A favourite of Elizabeth I, he may have planted the trees to curry favour with the monarch but it was a sound economic move anyway. Samuel Hartlib, an influential writer at the time who knew everyone from scientists and philosophers to farmers and fruit growers, claimed that in 1652 this orchard earned £1,000. Given that most growers claimed £10-15 per acre this seems a fanciful figure, but it does show that fruit growing was an activity worth pursuing.

John Gerard, in his *Herball* of 1597, recommended a number of varieties including 'Luke Warde's cherry', called after the man who brought them from Italy, 'Naples cherry' after the city of its origin, and another tree which he described as bearing very large cherries 'of a most pleasant taste, as witnesseth Mr. Bull, the Queenes Majesties Clockmaker, who did taste of the fruit (the tree bearing only one Cherry, which he did eate, but my selfe never tasted of it) at the impression hereof'. One hopes he had better luck in subsequent years.

William Lawson, in his *A New Orchard and Garden* of 1618, recommended that cherry trees should be grown on mounts alongside other ornamental fruits such as damsons and plums. For those with sufficiently large private gardens, cherries became very popular for both their ornamental and productive qualities; at her house in Wimbledon Queen Henrietta Maria, wife of Charles I, employed the French designer André Mollet to create a baroque design with avenues of cherry trees leading to a central fountain. The parliamentary surveyors who catalogued the garden recorded one hundred and fifty-seven cherry trees in the fruit and ornamental gardens.

Around this time settlers took their favourite cultivars with them to North America. There they found an abundance of wild fruits as well as cultivars that had travelled east from China and central Asia.

Some of these then made their way back to Britain.

One of the difficulties in tracing the history of any particular variety is that there was no universal system of classification until Carl Linnaeus established one in the eighteenth century. John Parkinson, apothecary to James I and later herbalist to Charles I, attempted to impose some order, as did John Tradescant, gardener to, among others, Charles I. It was an almost impossible task; a cherry thought to have been imported by John Tradescant in 1611 was first called 'John Tradescant' and later 'Tradescant's Heart'. It was identical to 'Noble' and was frequently wrongly listed as 'Archduke', which was in turn thought by some to be the 'Lusitanian', first mentioned by Pliny hundreds of years earlier.

In 1665 John Rea, a botanist and author, recommended sixteen varieties, including the 'Duke', later the 'May Duke', which was one of the intermediaries between sweet and sour cherries. The origins of these cherries are confusing; it seems likely that the name 'May Duke' is a corruption of Médoc suggesting that the fruits originated in France, but they were called *Anglais* or *Anglais Hâtive* (meaning 'Early English') by the French, indicating that perhaps they were bred in England. To further confuse matters, John Parkinson had mentioned a similar cherry called 'May' in 1629. In 1827 the Royal Horticultural Society published a list of the cherries it grew at Chiswick naming 246 varieties, but many of these may have been synonyms, for example the variety known as 'Wellington' may have originally been a 'Napoleon' but been given a change of name for patriotic reasons.

From the seventeenth century onwards the aim of most breeders was to cultivate smaller trees. Sweet cherries grew on trees that were too large for most private gardens and the huge trees were hard – and at times hazardous – to harvest. Many gardeners grew fruit trees in their walled gardens, either trained against the walls or along the dividing paths. Sour cherries, which grew on smaller trees, could be planted like this, but sweet cherries would simply overpower the area.

Throughout the nineteenth century new cultivars were introduced by men such as Thomas Andrew Knight ('Knight's Early Black' and 'Waterloo'), Thomas Rivers ('Early Rivers') and Thomas Ingram

('Frogmore Early'). They had mastered getting the fruit to ripen earlier but failed to reduce the size of the trees. Cherry orchards flourished in Kent, particularly along the River Medway where transport to London was quick and easy. With the advent of the railways, orchards were also planted in Hertfordshire, Buckinghamshire, Herefordshire and Worcestershire. In 1950 there were 5,200 hectares / 12,850 acres of traditional cherry orchards in Kent alone. In spring, signposts directed people along 'Blossom Routes'. In Devon, you could take a paddle steamer along the River Tamar to view the blossom, Cornish on one side, Devonian on the other. While young, the trees were interplanted with hops and hazels, and grass was planted between them as the trees grew larger. Sheep or cattle would then graze beneath the trees, creating an idyllic landscape. Sadly this scene is now rare.

Increasingly, in the second half of the twentieth century, the large trees proved uneconomic. The drier, warmer climates of France and Italy produced more reliable harvests and this meant that imported fruit was comparatively cheap in Britain. The noble stature of English cherry trees also began to tell against them. As 15 m / 50 feet was a fairly average height for the trees it meant that harvesting required specialized equipment and manpower. Long wooden ladders were precariously balanced amongst the branches, often inadvertently damaging the tender buds that would grow into the following year's crop. After the Second World War the specialized labour force needed for harvesting became both scarce and costly in Britain. While dwarfing rootstocks were developed for other fruits, cherries remained huge, and as a result many orchards were dug up and replaced with easier and more profitable fruits. On a tour of the cherry orchards at Brogdale (highly recommended), our guide told us that he remembered the long ladders still being used when he first started work there as a boy. Only the more experienced pickers were allowed up them. By 1994 there were a mere 550 hectares / 1,360 acres left. It may have been written in a different century and the orchard may have been lost for different reasons, but Mrs Ranevsky's heartfelt lament in Anton Chekhov's *The Cherry Orchard* seems just as applicable for our old cherry orchards: 'Oh, my orchard! – my dear,

my sweet, my beautiful orchard! My life, my youth, my happiness, goodbye! Goodbye!'

Rather surprisingly, 'Cherry-Pickers' refers not just to men on long ladders harvesting fruits but also to the 11th Hussars. They earned this nickname in 1811 when they were surprised by the French cavalry while picking cherries in an orchard in Spain. Later, in 1840, the name was altered to the Cherry-breeches or Cherrybums on account of the tight pink trousers which the officers wore.

In 1996 a group of Kentish growers travelled to America and saw trees growing on Gisela, a dwarfing rootstock developed in Germany. The smaller trees could be protected against late frosts and birds, and were easy to harvest, which meant that cherries were again recovering commercially. Even though we have lost the sight of the towering trees with clouds of blossom reaching up to the sky and fluffy white sheep mirroring the image below, it is good to know that cherries are again gracing the countryside.

Cherries in Language and Literature

Cherries are strewn through our language like so many delicious, brightly-coloured punctuation marks. We cherry pick the best jobs, take two bites of the cherry, and who can resist the small child winsomely begging 'pretty please, with a cherry on top'. The analogy 'life is a bowl of cherries' is employed so frequently as to have become a cliché, often applied ironically. The 1931 song *Life is Just a Bowl of Cherries* has been recorded by many artists including Judy Garland, Doris Day and Johnny Mathis, and Erma Bombeck's well-known memoir *If Life is a Bowl of Cherries, What Am I Doing in the Pits?*, whilst having nothing to do with cherries per se, has immortalized the phrase.

In Biblical times, cherries were the fruit of Paradise, symbols of both goodness and sweetness. Jesus gave St Peter cherries, telling him not to despise small things. They are often used to balance the evil of the apple, with Christ painted holding both fruits. A typical example, now in the Royal Collection, is *Virgin of the Cherries* (c.1540 after Joos

van Cleve) where an apple in the foreground symbolizes the fall of man while the cherries clutched by the baby Jesus represent the fruits of paradise. As in the Oriental blossom festivals, cherries in the West are also used by artists in paintings to symbolize the briefness and potential goodness of life. At the end of his anthology *Other Men's Flowers*, Field Marshal Lord Wavell added a small section entitled 'Outside the Gate'. It contained a single beautiful sonnet addressed to the 'Lady of the Cherries' in one of these Madonna paintings. It was written in April 1943 in the midst of the Second World War and ends with the lines:

> For all that loveliness, that warmth, that light.
> Blessed Madonna, I go back to fight.

The Cherry Tree Carol is based on a story in the Gospel of pseudo-Matthew, part of the New Testament Apocrypha and one of the gospels which aims to fill out details of the early life of Christ. There are many variations, but in most Joseph and the heavily-pregnant

Mary are walking in an orchard. She asks him to pick her a cherry whereupon he retorts, 'Let the father of thy baby gather cherries for thee.' From within the womb, Jesus asks the tree to bow down so his mother may reach the fruit. Joseph is, of course, suitably humbled when the tree dutifully lowers its boughs.

The cherry is also very much part of the language of seduction and just plain sex. The colour, lusciousness and transience of the ripe cherry has resulted in associations with maidenhood throughout literature. For the Elizabethans, adroit in wordplay, the association of cherry fruit with women and stones with men (stones was an early slang word for testicles) created a world of possibilities. William Shakespeare in his play within a play in *A Midsummer Night's Dream* has Thisbe declaim:

O Wall, full often has thou heard my moans
For parting my fair Pyramus and me!
My cherry lips have often kissed thy stones
Thy stones with lime and hair knit up in thee.

If you take into account the fact this scene has the wall played by a man dressed up as a wall you can understand how that one had the groundlings rolling around sniggering at the double meanings.

By the late nineteenth and early twentieth century, the linguistic association of cherries and virginity seems to have become even more explicit. From the nineteenth century onwards, deflowering was beginning to become directly linked with cherries with phrases such as break, get, pick or pop a cherry or cherry busting and cherry splitter entering common (very common we think) parlance. Cherries came to stand for young virginal girls. It is no accident that one of the tight-jersey-wearing Pink Ladies in the 1978 musical *Grease* is called Marty Maraschino ('What is your name?' 'Marty.' 'Marty what?' 'Marty Maraschino – you know, as in cherry'). Rock singer Joan Jett took control of the phrase in an early example of girl power when she and her band The Runaways had a hit with *Cherry Bomb,* belting out a song about an underage temptresses sung by a sixteen year old:

Hello Daddy, hello mom
I'm your ch-ch-ch-cherry bomb
Hello world! I'm your girl
I'm your ch-ch-ch-cherry bomb

On a higher level, lips and cherries are associated throughout sixteenth century poetry. Cherry lips were a common theme in poetry and song, with Thomas Campion combining both in his poem set to music 'There is a Garden in Her Face', whose refrain is 'there cherries grow, which none may buy, till "Cherry-ripe" themselves doe cry'. Robert Herrick's poem 'Cherry-Ripe' is typical of the period with romantic descriptions of Julia, the lady to whom much of his love poetry was addressed:

Cherrie-Ripe, Ripe, Ripe, I cry,
Full and faire ones; come and buy:
If so be, you ask me where
They doe grow? I answer, There,
Where my Julia's lips doe smile;
There's the Land, or Cherry-Ile:
Whose Plantations fully show
All the yeere, where Cherries grow.

Double cherries, used in early kissing games, are also a symbol of togetherness. Banned by many supermarkets (although surely not for their suggestive looks), double cherries make perfect earrings as many a little girl playing in the garden has found. D. H. Lawrence recognized this in his poem 'Cherry Robbers', where he paints a revealing picture of a rural miss: 'Against the haystack a girl stands laughing at me, Cherries hung round her ears.'

Many authors use cherry orchards as trysting places. Understandably so, as cherry trees are beautiful and if he doesn't turn up you can console yourself with a cherry feast. In Leo Tolstoy's novella *Family Happiness* this leads to a marriage proposal, whereas in D. H. Lawrence's *Sons and Lovers* an eight-year relationship is consummated after some seductive fruit picking. Less happily, the fleeting nature of things can be mirrored in the cherry blossoms. In Anton Chekov's *The Cherry Orchard*, a Russian landowner returns to her estate when it is to be sold up to pay debts. The themes of futility and hopelessness are echoed in the sounds of the cherry orchard being cut down at the end of the play. Interestingly, Anton Chekov himself saw *The Cherry Orchard* as a farce or comedy, well, he was Russian…

Mary Poppins, everyone's idea of a perfect nanny, takes charge of the children of Cherry Tree Lane and Enid Blyton's *The Children of Cherry Tree Farm* tells the story of four children spending a year in the country. Cherry pies are munched on gleefully throughout children's literature, but for an insight into the true pride of baking cherry pies we need to look further afield to Truman Capote's *In Cold Blood*, which includes a fabulous description:

> Nancy and her protégée, Jolene Katz were satisfied with their morning's work; indeed, the latter, a thin thirteen-year-old, was agog with pride. For the longest while, she stared at the blue-ribbon winner, the oven-hot cherries simmering under the crisp lattice crust, and then she was really overcome, and, hugging Nancy, asked, 'Honest, did I really make that myself?' Nancy laughed, returned the embrace, and assured her that she had – with a little help…Joelene cut a piece of pie. 'Boy!' She said, wolfing it down, 'I'm going to make one of those every day, seven days a week'.

Try our cherry pie recipe on page 131 and see if you have the same reaction.

Cherries mostly have positive connotations, however a more sinister view seems to emerge for some, as in Magda Szabo's *The Door*, where the writer watches her mysterious neighbour bottling cherries:

> Emerence had turned her attention to the cherries, and was hauling out the same cauldron in which she had been boiling

sheets the day we first met…The stream of cherries tumbled into the cauldron. By now we were in the world of myth – the pitted cherries separating out, the juice beginning to flow like blood from a wound, and Emerence, calmness personified, standing over the cauldron in her black apron, her eyes in shadow under the hooded headscarf.

Who needs a jam pan?

CHERRY FESTIVALS AND GAMES

The cherry harvest comes close to midsummer and was always regarded as a good excuse for a celebration. Cherry fairs tended to be a cross between a market and a party, and in medieval times they gained a reputation for bawdiness, possibly because of the slightly seductive nature of the fruit, or perhaps the fact that the weather was warm enough to make lying beneath the trees with one's loved one a practical option. Cherry fairs usually take place in July, with Cherry Pie Sunday, traditionally held in Buckinghamshire on the first Sunday in August, extending the festivities.

Robert Herrick's poems almost form a manual for seventeenth-century cherry games, even though love rather than fairground entertainment is his primary concern:

'Chop-Cherry'
Thou gav'st me leave to kisse;
Thou gav'st me leave to woo;
Thou mad'st me thinke by this,
And that, thou lov'dst me too.

But I shall ne'er forget,
How for to make thee merry;
Thou mad'st me chop, but yet,
Another snapt the Cherry.

In the game, each player attempts to eat a dangling cherry, either hanging from the tree or a string.

Cherry Pit, Cherry Stone or Cheriston was another popular game. Cherry stones were thrown or spat into a small pit or hole, the player accurately aiming the most stones being the winner. A variation can be played with marbles, where the aim is to use your selected marble to push others into the pit. Again Robert Herrick has used the game for his own ends:

'Cherry-Pit'
Julia and I did lately sit
Playing for sport, at Cherry-pit:
She threw; I cast; and having thrown,
I got the Pit, and she the Stone.

In William Shakespeare's *Twelfth Night* Malvolio is taunted by Sir Toby Belch 'What man, 'tis not for gravity to play at cherry-pit with Satan'.

CHERRY USES IN THE KITCHEN...AND BEYOND

Various ancient beliefs are associated with cherry trees. The bark is strong smelling and was reputed to ward off the plague if placed above the door. In Scotland, bird cherry trees are known as hagberries and are associated with witches, although the wood could also provide protection: a walker with a bird cherry stick would apparently never get lost in the frequent mists that descended on the unwary.

Despite the fact that in Shetland the cherry is called the merry tree, and that cherries have a longstanding association with love, in the North Country of England it is considered unlucky to use cherry blossom at weddings. This is possibly an extension of the superstition that May is an unlucky month ('Marry in May and you will surely rue the day').

Cuckoos and cherries are closely linked in tradition and reputedly a cuckoo must eat three good meals of cherries before he is allowed to

CHERRIES & MULBERRIES

cease singing. If you want to use the fruit to determine your lifespan you should chant:

> Cuckoo cherry tree
> Come down and tell to me
> How many years I have to live?

Each child (or adult) then chooses a branch in turn and shakes it; the number of fruits to fall will determine the number of years they will live. If on the other hand you wish to rely on the bird then try:

> Cuckoo, cuckoo, cherry-tree,
> Good bird prithee tell to me,
> How many years I am to see?

Despite this one scanning better, the number of times the bird repeats the call is the clincher and we feel a well-chosen, fully-laden tree branch may yield a better result.

As well as determining our lifespan, cherries can also foretell our professions, or that of our future husbands, how we will marry and where we will live. Simply eat some cherries and count the stones:

> Tinker, tailor, soldier, sailor,
> Rich man, poor man, beggar man, thief.
> Silk, satin, muslin, rags,
> Coach, carriage, wheelbarrow, cart.
> Big house, little house, pigsty, barn
> This year, next year, sometime, never.

Variations include a palace or a cottage, with a gentleman, an apothecary or a ploughboy being nineteenth century alternatives for one's career/husband.

Cherries have appeared in recipe books from the earliest times, most commonly candied, dried, as wine or in brandy. They were primarily used in sweet rather than savoury preparations although

Germany, along with the superlative Black Forest Gâteau, also offers a range of sweet and sour dishes and pickles, most often pairing cherries with game. In Alsace, France, there is a cherry soup served over squares of fried bread which is traditionally eaten on Christmas Eve. Indeed throughout Northern Europe cherry soups have been staples. However as we, and more importantly our tasters, regard fruit soups as an abomination we have not included any recipes here.

Eaten since medieval times, cherries in Britain have long been associated with festivals often held at the end of the cherry-picking season in late summer. Traditionally small cherry pies or turnovers called 'bumpers' were baked and eaten at the festival, along with a pint of ale. These are a form of sweet pasty using short crust pastry and filled with stoned cherries and sugar. The cries of London street sellers, including 'Cherries so ripe and so round, the best in the market found, they're only a penny a pound, so who will buy?' have echoed in the capital and beyond since the sixteenth century. Henry Mayhew included cherry sellers in his ground-breaking study of working people in Victorian London, *London Labour and the London Poor*. As well as being sold by weight, cherries were also sold on sticks with bunches tied to the sticks with fine thread.

According to Sir Kenelm Digby, in his delightfully-named *The Closet of Sir Kenelm Digby Opened* (1669), one should eat morello cherries for pleasure and black cherries for health. Morellos are very dark cherries, often called black now. The name may mean 'little Moor', referring to the fact that they reached Britain via Spain. Historically cherries were valued for their cleansing properties; it was widely believed that they would eliminate toxins and excess fluid from the body. They had a reputation for being easily digested, acting as an appetizer or purgative according to how many you ate. They were used to relieve rheumatism and arthritis and cherry stalk tea was believed to ease gout. (Look on page 40 and see how some of these beliefs persist today.)

In his herbal of 1653, Nicholas Culpeper states that sweet and sour cherries both have their uses, either fresh or dried, but it is the gum he particularly recommends. Dissolved in wine it eases coughs, colds and sore throats (even today cough mixture is often cherry flavoured, although more to make it palatable than to increase efficacy). It 'mendeth the colour in the face, sharpeneth the eye-sight, provoketh appetite and helpeth to break and expel the stone'. It used to be chewed as a gum by children and could also be used as an adhesive. Dissolved in water, cherry gum was a popular treatment for sore nipples during nursing in the seventeenth and eighteenth century.

John Nott, whose book was a compilation of recipes he had collected from 1650-1715, included conserves, preserves, marmalade and paste using cherries. In 1747 Hannah Glasse added pies to the cherry repertoire in *The Art of Cookery Made Plain and Easy,* and Eliza Acton a hundred years later ignored the pies and tarts but included several recipes for dried cherries, including a 'superior receipt' which involved more time and sugar (in our opinion extra sugar so often results in a superior receipt). In 1861 Mrs Beeton listed cherry brandy, cherry jam, cherry sauce and cherry tart, firmly establishing the cherry's position in the kitchen.

Cherries really came to the fore with the advent of patisserie and no reputable patissier would dream of missing a cherry tart or cherry lattice from their line-up. The greatest patissier of all, Auguste Escoffier, even developed a special cherry dessert for Queen Victoria's Silver Jubilee (see Cherry Jubilee on page 133).

Griottines are a French cherry specialty which have spawned an institution. Traditionally, long stalked *griotte* cherries were enclosed with kirsch in a chocolate shell and eaten off of the stalk. Once the preserve of Franche-Comté on the eastern border of France with Switzerland, the sheer perfection of the combination has resulted in cherry liqueur chocolates now being consumed worldwide.

The popular maraschino cherry originated several centuries ago in northeast Italy and the neighbouring Balkans, where the local Marasca cherry was preserved in its own liqueur for eating over the winter. Our favourite brand, Luxardo, still uses a traditional family recipe. Girolamo Luxardo was a Genoese sent to Zara on the Dalmatian coast as Sardinian consul in 1817. His wife Maria Canevari was interested in old medieval recipes and perfected the 'rosolio maraschino', a liqueur originally produced in Dalmatian convents. Girolamo founded a distillery in 1821 to produce her recipe commercially. He gained an endorsement from the Emperor of Austria and today's bottles still carry the imprint 'Privilegiata Fabbrica Maraschino Excelsior'. At the end of the First World War, Zara was absorbed into Italy and the distillery continued to flourish. However during the Second World War, labour shortages and repeated Anglo-American bombing almost completely destroyed the plant. After the war the area was occupied by Tito's communist parties, and most of the Italian population fled or were killed, including several members of the Luxardo family. However in 1947 Giorgio Luxardo built a distillery in the Veneto region and today the sixth generation of the family is back, creating Maraschino and related premium products.

The original large trees provided wood for furniture as well as fruit. When polished it had a beautiful shine similar to pale mahogany. In the days when people smoked, cherry-wood pipes were popular and in Cockney rhyming slang 'cherry ripe' means 'pipe', although here it is the rhyme rather than the material which makes the association. Oil from the seed is used in many cosmetics and the black fruits can be used to dye fabric, particularly wool.

Cherry Festivals

UK
Brogdale Cherry Festival, Brogdale Road, Faversham, Kent ME13 8XZ
Cherry Pie Fayre, Seer Green, Buckinghamshire
Black Cherry Fair, Chertsey, Surrey

USA
National Cherry Festival, Traverse City, Michigan
Leona Valley Cherry Parade and Festival, California

THE STORY OF MULBERRIES

A fruit of exquisite, if elusive, taste that comes from a handsome tree.

(David C. Stuart, *The Kitchen Garden*)

From the steppes of Central Asia and the mountain ranges of eastern China, mulberries travelled to Europe and the Americas, bringing luscious dark fruits and priceless silks. There are three main types of mulberry: black, white and red. Black mulberries (*Morus nigra*) are also known as Persian and are the trees that, on the whole, give the best fruit. Confusingly the berries of white mulberries (*M. alba*) come in a range of colours, from white to dark purple, but they tend to lack flavour; according to Alexandre Dumas they are 'used for feeding farm animals, which eat them with great pleasure'. With these trees it is the leaves that are important, providing food for the humble but industrious silkworm. Red mulberries (*M. rubra*) are native to North America and are renowned as ornamental trees, but their berries tend to be tart and their leaves unsuitable for silkworms.

The Name

The name *Morus* comes from the Latin *mora*, meaning delay. Mulberries are often called the wise fruit, first by Pliny in his *Natural History*, as they do not start to grow in spring until the danger of frost is over: 'Of all the cultivated trees, the mulberry is the last to bud, which it never does until the cold weather is past…but when it begins to put forth buds, it despatches the business in one night and that with so much force that their breaking forth may be clearly heard.'

Later in the seventeenth century, John Evelyn offered more practical advice regarding when it was safe to bring orange trees out from their winter protection in conservatories: 'observe the mulberry tree, when it begins to put forth and open the leaves (be it earlier or later) bring your oranges etc., boldly out of the conservatory'.

Black and white mulberries are separate species but Ovid, in his *Metamorphoses*, has a more fanciful origin for the black fruits in the tale of Pyramus and Thisbe. The two young lovers decided to elope, arranging to meet beneath a white mulberry tree. Thisbe arrived first but was frightened by the roar of a lion and ran away, dropping her cloak. The lion, bloodstained from a recent kill, mauled the cloak and then left. Pyramus arrived, was devastated at the death of his love and stabbed himself. When Thisbe returned she found him dying and, distraught, she took his sword and killed herself. Ever after their blood has turned the white berries blood red.

Ancient Times

Black mulberry seeds have been found in early Egyptian tombs and were cultivated by both the Greeks and the Romans. The tree was dedicated to Minerva, the goddess of wisdom and Horace recommended eating mulberries at the end of a meal as a way of keeping healthy during the summer heat. As well as eating the fresh fruits, the Romans made mulberries into wine and syrup. Pliny warned that the juice of ripe fruits would stain the hands, but that the stain could be washed out with the juice of unripe fruits. At Pompeii there is a black mulberry depicted in the peristyle of the House of the Bull, and mulberry leaves are included in a mosaic in the House of the Faun. Black mulberries may also have ancient origins in western Asia and Eastern Europe. In prehistoric Armenia and Kurdistan they were dried and made into cakes to eat during winter and also reputedly used as currency.

MULBERRIES IN BRITAIN

Mulberries were almost certainly brought to England by the Romans and, as the fruits do not travel well, it is likely that trees were planted. Excavations of Roman sites in London found mulberry pips dating from the first century AD. The trees are long-lived and grow true from seed, so it is probable that trees planted by the Romans, or their seedlings, would have survived until Anglo-Saxon times when they were called 'mon-beams'.

Mulberries often survived in monastery gardens throughout the Middle Ages and the berries became popular at Tudor banquets. In the 1551 edition of his *Herball,* William Turner's description of the fruit gives the impression that it was already fairly widespread.

The trees quickly develop a gnarled appearance, making them look old beyond their years, but they are also very long-lived. The Drapers' Company, one of the Twelve Great Livery Companies in the City of London, has a long history of planting mulberry trees in their garden and it is claimed that a tree planted in 1364 was fruiting until 1969. Each year a mulberry pie would be given to the Lord Mayor, made with fruit from their trees.

The mulberries at Syon Park, west London, include a tree planted in 1548, probably the oldest surviving tree in Britain. The mulberry at Kew gardens was a cutting from one of these trees and is scathingly regarded as 'much younger' by the staff at Syon House. Many venerable trees survive but sadly not the one that William Shakespeare planted at Stratford-upon-Avon. In the 1750s the Reverend Francis Gastrell, who owned the house, cut the tree down as he was fed up with the constant stream of visitors. A tree of a similar age in the

Chelsea Physic Garden in London was dug up during the Second World War to make way for a bomb shelter, but cuttings were taken and many of these have thrived; the one in the garden already looks suitably ancient.

John Gerard, in his *Herball* of 1597, describes red and white mulberries but says they 'grow plentifully in Italy and other hot regions, where they doe maintain great woods and groves of them that their Silke wormes may feed thereon'. This, as will be seen, is the problem at the root of the failure of the attempts to produce silk in England.

SILK

Mulberries have been cultivated in China for silk for over five thousand years. The fabric probably arrived in Europe around 330 BC, brought there along the Silk Road, with other goods from the east, as a result of Alexander's eastern campaigns. Pliny described the fabric as showing the person through it, rather than covering and hiding their form, and Emperor Tiberius passed a law making it illegal for men to wear the fabric as he felt it was effeminate. Virgil, Aristotle and Pliny all connected the fabric with silkworms, but none made the link to mulberry trees. Myths regarding the production of silk abounded, including that which said the silkworm made its cocoon in the eyebrows of a beautiful maiden.

The thread is spun by the Chinese silkworm (*Bombyx mori*), which will only eat mulberry leaves. Silk was (and still is) a valuable commodity; in 524 it was sold in Europe for its weight in gold. The Chinese guarded the secret of its production and heavy penalties were inflicted on anyone caught smuggling the trees, seeds or silkworms abroad. The first place outside China to practice sericulture was the Kingdom of Khotan in Central Asia, in 140 BC. According to the story, the King of Khotan married a Chinese Imperial princess and before the wedding he warned his bride-to-be that if she wanted to continue to wear silk she would need to enable him to produce it for her. Legend has it that she smuggled out mulberry seeds and silkworm eggs in an elaborate headdress.

Silk production spread to India and along the Silk Road. In the sixth century two Persian monks travelled to China and smuggled silkworms out hidden inside a bamboo cane. They took them to Constantinople and from there the secrets of silk spread across mainland Europe, first to Italy, after the Sack of Constantinople in 1204 forced many craftsmen to flee, and then to Lyons in France which, in 1540, was granted a monopoly by François I.

In France, Henri IV (1589-1610) planted mulberries in the Tuileries as part of his building and gardening projects. Under his instruction over 15,000 trees were planted in the gardens. Most of these were white and were pruned for maximum silk production.

Silk in Britain

Many silk weavers came to England in the sixteenth and early seventeenth centuries to escape religious persecution on the continent. It became a thriving industry, but one which was dependent on expensive imports. James I was determined to free Britain from the Chinese monopoly and in 1606 he granted a patent whereby one-year-old mulberry saplings were to be imported and sold at no more than a penny each. In November 1609 he sent out instructions to the Lord Lieutenants of the counties that mulberry trees were to be planted throughout the country. Trees would be sent out the following spring, 'at the rate of three farthings a plant or at six shillings the hundred containing five score plants'. For the less well-off, packets of seeds were available. William Stallenge, later the Keeper of the King's Mulberry Gardens, published books on the care of both the trees and silkworms.

The failure of this venture tends to be blamed on the fact that black, rather than white, mulberries were planted, but there were valid reasons for the decision. At the time, it was known that white mulberries produced the finest silk, as the leaves which the worms eat appeared earlier and were more nutritious than those on black-fruited trees. John Parkinson summed up the problem: 'Some are confident that the leaves of the blacke [mulberry] will doe as much good as the white: but that respect must be had to change your seede, because therein lyeth the greatest mysterie.' As white mulberries need a warm climate, it was probably felt that planting black mulberries was a compromise that had a chance of success in England. It is worth remembering that at this time the climate in England was considerably colder than it is now. It must be said that the royal gardeners and advisors were correct, as no white mulberry trees survive from this time whereas many black ones are still growing healthily. There are trees at Charlton House in Greenwich, the Queen's Orchard in Greenwich Park, Cheyne Walk in Chelsea, west London, and a whole host more growing in the private gardens of the houses and flats that have sprung up on the sites of earlier orchards. Mulberry Walk in Chelsea refers to one of the mulberry gardens King James I planted.

Part of the garden of St James' Palace was planted with mulberries, a four-acre site on the area now occupied by the garden of Buckingham Palace. Inigo Jones was commissioned to design a silkworm house for the royal palace of Oatlands by the Thames, near Weybridge in Surrey. The Royal family took a keen interest in the project, hand feeding the silkworms, but in the end only sufficient silk was produced to make the Queen a taffeta dress to wear on the King's birthday. Later attempts to grow silk were undeterred by this failure, in particular the Raw Silk Undertaking founded by John Appletree in 1718. At first it seemed successful, with trees planted in Chelsea Park (the area bounded by the Kings Road, Fulham Road, Park Walk and Church Street). However, by 1724 the business had failed and John Appletree was declared bankrupt. It is not clear why it failed so suddenly, but the removal of import tax on raw silk in 1721 cannot have helped. In 1876 the park had gone, replaced by the Elm Park estate where, in the private gardens, mulberries continue to grow.

Long after the silk industry died, many of the trees remained in private gardens and in the popular Mulberry Garden. John Evelyn visited on 10 May 1654 and wrote in his diary: 'My lady Gerrard treated us at Mulberry Garden, now the onely place of refreshment about the towne for persons of the best quality to be exceedingly cheated at; Cromwell and his partisans having shut up and seized on Spring Garden, which till now had been the usual rendezvous for the ladys and gallants at this season.' Samuel Pepys describes them on an evening in 20 May 1668: 'I...walked over the park to the Mulberry Garden, where I never was before; and find it a very silly place, worse than Spring Garden, and but little company and those a

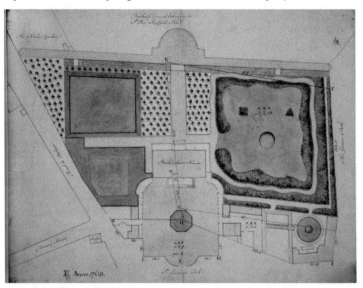

Buckingham House Gardens 1760 CRES 2/1648 (The National Archives).

Cherries & Mulberries

rascally, whoring, roguing sort of people; only a wilderness here that is somewhat pretty, but rude. Did not stay to drink, but walked an hour.' In 1705 the Gardens were incorporated into the grounds of the newly built Buckingham House, later Buckingham Palace, which still holds the National Collection of the trees.

SILK IN AMERICA

In the early seventeenth century the Virginia Company encouraged settlers to set up a silk industry using native mulberry trees. In 1621 silkworms were shipped from Britain and books on sericulture followed. The project was more successful than it had been in Britain and sufficient silk was produced for Charles II's coronation robes.

In the nineteenth century 'mulberry mania' hit America when a new variety of mulberry arrived in the country. *Morus* var. *multicaulis* had come from China via France and caused a stir similar to the tulip mania in seventeenth century Europe, when prices shot up and fortunes were made or lost. The new tree was reputed to grow faster than the white mulberry, which would lead to quicker profits. Millions of trees were planted and the old ones dug up. Too late, it was discovered that the silkworms didn't really like the new trees.

MULBERRIES IN THE NURSERY

Mulberry trees are known to most children, by name if not by looks, from the rhyme *Here We Go Round the Mulberry Bush*. The rhyme describes a number of everyday activities such as washing and getting dressed which would have been acted out by the children. Some versions even included the way ladies and gentlemen walk. There were many similar songs throughout Europe in the nineteenth century, with bramble or juniper bushes also being the plant danced round. It may be a traditional song, but the women's prison at Wakefield claims it as theirs. There was, and still is, a mulberry tree in the prison yard and their claim is that the women prisoners sang to entertain their children as they exercised round the tree.

USES

Elephants have often been used in war, their sheer bulk proving a useful weapon. What seems surprising is this reference to elephants being shown mulberries, though quite how it encouraged them to fight is unclear: 'Then the king rising very early marched fiercely with his host towards Bathzacharias, where his armies made them ready to battle, and sounded the trumpets. And to the end they might provoke the elephants to fight, they showed them the blood of grapes and mulberries.' (1 Maccabees 6 verses 33-4.) At the time it was probably believed, incorrectly, that the colour would have encouraged the elephants to fight because it was the colour of blood.

The fruits of the black mulberry make a good strong dye, as unwary pickers often discover. During the Middle Ages the juice was used as a dye and also to make wine or give colour and flavour to wines which needed 'improving'. *Murrey* was a purée of mulberries used in cooking. Gerard says the berries will quench thirst but contain little nourishment. According to him the bark, steeped in vinegar, will ease toothache, a cure taken from Dioscorides who recommended also using the leaves and 'that about harvest time there issueth out of the root a juyce, which the next day after is found to be hard'.

The wood is both hard and attractive and is valued for cabinetry and fence posts; according to John Evelyn it was used by carpenters, wheelwrights and even shipbuilders.

OTHER MULBERRIES

The paper mulberry (*Broussonetia papyrifera*) was used to make paper in Japan and East Asia. The fruits of this tree are edible and turn an attractive orangey-red when ripe. Paper is made by soaking and smoothing the bark, but the leaves feel so papery it would almost seem possible to write on them too. Probably first made by the Chinese, it is still used in Japan for washi or high-quality paper, lanterns and umbrellas. It is also called the tapa cloth tree as many Pacific islands use the inner bark to make ceremonial costumes, bedding and bags.

The Indian mulberry (*Morinda citrifolia*) is actually a member of the coffee family. It grows in the tropics and Australia and bears flowers and fruits throughout the year.

The fruit has a pungent smell when ripening, and is often known as cheese fruit or even vomit fruit. It is also sometimes called starvation fruit as it is a staple food, either raw or cooked, in some Pacific islands, while in Thai cuisine the leaves are cooked with coconut milk. They are allegedly one of the fruits that the Polynesians took from southeast Asia to Hawaii. The bark produces a brownish-purplish dye and the roots produce a yellow dye, both of which are used to colour cloth.

During the Middle Ages the Peloponnese peninsula in Greece was called Morea. This may have been because mulberries were grown in the area or, as the Byzantine scholar Steven Runciman suggests, that the shape of the Peloponnese resembles a mulberry leaf.

Mulberry was also the unlikely-sounding name for the prefabricated ports that were deployed during the Second World War. They consisted of flexible steel roadways on concrete pontoons. Breakwaters provided protection and meant that large ships could be safely unloaded. They were towed across the Channel to Normandy to help get supplies to the Allied armies in 1944 after the D-Day landings. The name was chosen simply because it was next on the British Admiralty's list of names available for warships.

HEALTH

Ille salubris aestates peraget, qui nigris prandia moris finiet.
(A man will pass his summers in health who will finish his lunch with black mulberries.)

(Horace, *Satires*)

The dark red colour of both cherries and mulberries is a beacon to good health. All berries are good for you (we know, cherries are technically drupes but cherries rhymes with berries, bear with us...) and, as a general rule, the darker the colour, the better the benefit. Dark coloured fruits usually contain more beneficial carotenoids and phenolic compounds than their paler cousins. The benefits are often contained in the skins, so fruits you don't need to peel (and you would have to be mad to try to peel a mulberry or indeed a cherry) are the best choice. Carotenoids and phenolic compounds are rich sources of antioxidants and antioxidants help counteract the deleterious effects of ageing and pollutants, keeping you looking and feeling better for longer.

Let's look at the specific benefits of both fruits separately.

Cherries & Mulberries

CHERRIES

Vitamins

Cherries are an excellent source of vitamins C, A and E. Vitamin C has been long associated with the prevention of colds and flu, but it is also essential for the growth and repair of body tissues and the immune system more generally, the formation of collagen, the absorption of iron, and the maintenance of cartilage, bones and teeth. A person's daily requirement of vitamin C is between 65 and 90 milligrams (depending on who you read) and a 150 gram portion of cherries can provide up to a quarter of this. Indeed, one of the richest sources of vitamin C naturally available is the acerola or West Indian cherry, a fruit which contains 65 times more vitamin C than an orange. Despite its looks (it looks like a cherry) and its name (it is also known as the Barbados cherry) this tropical fruit which originated from Mexico and South America is botanically *Malpighia punicifolia* (syn. *M. emarginata, M. glabra*), so are far removed from our *Prunus* fruits.

Vitamin A has benefits for eye health and works on the immune system and to improve cell growth.

A and E together enhance libido in both men and women. Vitamin A boosts testosterone and oestrogen levels, whereas E reputedly feeds sexual appetite and can increase men's semen volume. Move over Oyster Rockefeller, we see Cherries Casanova as the new aphrodisiac de nos jours.

Anti-Cancer Claims

Ellagic acid and queritrin, both found in cherries, are considered as cancer blockers. Queritrin is a natural anticarcinogenic and ellagic acid can effectively prevent the proliferation of certain carcinogens and inhibit the development of cancer. Both are powerful antioxidants. Early animal trials have suggested perillyl alcohol, derived from the essential oils in cherries, can act as a cancer blocker. Although this is yet to be tested on humans it is an area which shows promise and has been flagged for further research.

Joint and Muscle Benefits

Traditionally we associate gout with elderly, port-drinking gentlemen, but in fact anyone can suffer from this painful condition. Gout is caused by a build-up of uric acid in the body which causes crystals to form in the joints and surrounding tissue. Most commonly it occurs in the big toe, knee or ankle. Recent small-scale trials by the Boston University School of Medicine and the Philadelphia VA Medical Centre have both indicated benefits to gout sufferers from the regular eating of cherries or drinking cherry juice. It seems that cherries reduce the blood level of uric acid whilst increasing the levels of anthocyanin compounds. Anthocyanins are antioxidants with powerful anti-inflammatory properties.

These same properties are also reputed to have beneficial effects on sufferers of osteoarthritis, who report decreased pain and stiffness when regularly consuming cherries. About a cup of cherries (around twenty), two 8 oz bottles of cherry juice or two teaspoons of concentrated juice need to be consumed daily for noticeable effect.

The anti-inflammatory and antioxidant benefits of cherries can be as strong for the healthy. Studies of long distance runners have suggested that athletes who drink tart cherry juice (as ever it is tart rather than sweet cherries which confer the benefit) before exercise experienced less pain and muscle damage. A study by the University of Michigan further suggested that the anthocyanins in cherries act like pain killers in the body, with one serving of tart cherries having a similar pain-killing effect to 1.4 grams of aspirin. Another study, this time by London Bank University, observed that athletes drinking diluted cherry concentrate regained 90% of their normal muscle tone within 24 hours.

Skin Benefits

The antioxidant and vitamin content of cherries has knock-on benefits for the skin. Vitamin C has recognized anti-ageing effects conferred by antioxidants. In particular it is believed to prevent, or at least retard, the formation of lines, wrinkles and age spots on the skin, and to counter the ageing effects of sun and weather on the complexion.

A simple but effective cleanser can be made by crushing a cup of cherries and applying the resulting paste to your face. Your skin will be left feeling smooth and soft and the acidic properties in the fruit helps to dissolve away dead skin cells. A side benefit is of course that you can always lick it off if you feel a little peckish.

Drinking cherry juice has been promoted as a treatment for acne and rosacea. In this case it is the black, rather than the tart, cherry juice you are looking for, as this is higher in vitamins A and C. Vitamin A is considered to have antibacterial properties which remove toxins from the blood and eliminate bacteria below the skin.

MELATONIN

Cherries are a natural source of melatonin which can promote improved sleep patterns. Melatonin travels easily across the blood-brain barrier and has a soothing effect, calming down nervous system irritability. The benefit is more noticeable in tart than sweet cherries. It has been suggested that drinking a glass of tart cherry juice 30 minutes before your evening meal boosts melatonin levels which regulate sleep cycles and result in a better quality and longer sleep. Melatonin is also a factor in countering jet lag, so cherry juice or fresh cherries could be your ideal in-flight snack.

GLYCEMIC INDEX

The glycemic index of a food is a numerical value which indicates how 'sugary' a food is. Foods with a high glycemic index cause increases in blood sugar, whilst those with lower ratings have minimal impact. As a guide, a rating from mid fifties to sixties is considered average, whilst anything above seventy is high. Foods below fifty-five are considered low and to have insignificant impact on blood sugar levels. In comparison with many other fruits cherries have a very low glycemic index (22), making them a preferred snack choice for diabetics in search of a fruit fix. Remember that these glycemic index ratings apply to the raw fruit, if you stew your cherries in sugar syrup or turn to bottled or canned products then they will not have the same benefits.

Blood Pressure and Stroke

Cherries contribute to a healthy diet and aid in minimising the risk from hypertension and stroke. The anthocyanins in cherries may activate PPARs (peroxisome proliferator-activated receptors, since you ask, those transcription factors which regulate genes assisting in maintaining energy balance). They work on glucose metabolism reducing the risk of high cholesterol, blood pressure issues and diabetes. The potassium content in cherries (between 90 and 222 milligrams per 100 grams depending on the type of cherry and its method of preparation) regulates heart rate and blood pressure, decreasing the risk of hypertension. A Northumbria University study reported that participants who drank 60 ml of cherry concentrate diluted with water experienced a 7% drop in their blood pressure levels over three hours. This led them to conclude that regular consumption of cherry juice could reduce the risk of stroke by 38%.

MULBERRIES

Mulberries share many of the antioxidant benefits of cherries. As sources of vitamins C and K, along with potassium, calcium and iron, they are little power packs. The potassium helps boost energy levels, repair cell damage (it's those antioxidants again) and boost the immune system.

Digestive Health

Mulberries are a good source of fibre, one serving providing 10% of your recommended daily intake. Fibre helps move food through the digestive tract more efficiently, reducing the risk of constipation, bloating and cramps.

Historically, a syrup made from mulberries is recognised in the British Pharmacopoeia as being an expectorant, a laxative and an effective gargle for sore throats. Gerard recommends it, stating: 'The barke of the root is bitter, hot and drie, and hath a scoring faculty, the decoction hereof doth open the stoppings of the liver and spleen, it purgeth the belly and driveth forth worms.' Nice…

BLOOD AND CIRCULATION BENEFITS

More recent research suggests that mulberries are a superfood (isn't everything? In our view, chocolate is a superfood, possibly the only superfood). Mulberries contain resveratrol, widely believed to be an anti-cancer agent with healthy heart benefits and anti-inflammatory properties. It acts as a vasodilator, relaxing the blood vessels and making them less prone to clots which can cause strokes and heart attacks. Resveratrol is rarely found in foods but does occur in grapes. The much-lauded 'French paradox', where the French seem to follow an enviable lifestyle gorging on confit, camembert and frites with everything but not gaining weight and enjoying remarkable longevity, is credited to the presence of resveratrol from grapes in red wine. Other sources of resveratrol include blueberries, sprouted peanuts, cocoa and…ta-dah…mulberries. The anti-inflammatory benefits are further believed to help alleviate arthritis and arteriosclerosis and postpone the onset of Alzheimer's and Parkinson's disease.

It is unusual for fruit to provide a source of iron but mulberries are an exception. The iron content of mulberries is helpful in enhancing the production of red blood cells. Red blood cells assist in the distribution of oxygen to vital tissues and organs, and improve their function and efficiency.

Mulberries are known to improve blood circulation and this, coupled with their anti-inflammatory properties, helps lower blood pressure making one less susceptible to blood clots and strokes.

The bark, leaves and roots of mulberries (young twigs and roots, not those from older wood), contain flavonoids which have diuretic and expectorant properties and reputedly increase insulin levels and decrease blood glucose. The Chinese recognised this and have long used extract of mulberry to treat diabetes. They were drawing on chemical compounds in the leaves, which worked to suppress the high blood sugar level spike (hyperglycaemia) which can occur after a carbohydrate rich meal. Because mulberry extract has a marked effect on lowering blood sugar it needs to be approached with caution by those who need to carefully monitor and control their blood sugar levels.

Mulberry Tea

Mulberry leaves have tranquillizing effects and have been recommended for tisanes (indeed in Thailand we tried some delicious White Mulberry Tea). In traditional Chinese medicine it is recommended to assist in the improvement of vision, cleanse the liver and expel wind. The mulberry leaf has 25 times more calcium than milk so it could be helpful for those with dairy intolerances. Lest you start swigging it back though, remember moderation in everything. In quantity, it has been suggested that the leaves can cause hallucinations, headaches and tummy upsets, so maybe limit yourself to a couple of cups.

Bone Health

The presence of calcium and iron, plus traces of phosphorous and magnesium, means that mulberries are good for bone health and may act against the effects of osteoarthritis and other deleterious bone conditions.

Eye Health

Zeaxanthin, a carotenoid found in mulberries and other plants including saffron, bell peppers and corn, contributes to their distinctive strong colours and has significant benefits for eye health. It can reduce stress on ocular cells and prevent damage to the retina, such as that caused by macular degeneration and cataracts.

Skin Health

If you steep the leaves of mulberries in olive or coconut oil you can use the resultant decoction as a topical treatment for dry or irritated skin. In fact, mulberry extract is frequently used in anti-ageing skin creams. You can do your own home facial by boiling mulberry leaves in water, placing the concoction in a wide bowl, putting a towel over your head and leaning over the steam. Rinse your face afterwards with cold water.

IN THE GARDEN

MULBERRY

No man can have fair Plants unless he love them…
it is the Affection of the Master which animates them,
and renders them strong and vigorous.
(Sieur Le Gendre, *The Manner of Ordering Fruit Trees*)

To get the best cherries and mulberries you really need to grow your own. Cherries do not travel well, mulberries not at all. They are both easy to grow and require less space than you might imagine.

Cherries are divided into sweet fruits, sour, tart or acid fruits (called sour from here onwards) and dukes, which are a cross between the two. The trees are now available on a variety of rootstocks which means they can be grown to suit most spaces and will thrive as trained plants or in a container. The spectacular spring blossom can be pink or white and the fruits can be any colour from yellow to purply-black. Sour cherries are important, not only for their wonderful cooking fruit, but because alone of nearly all the fruit trees they will thrive in shade or against north-facing walls. The blossom is not quite as amazing as that of dessert cherries, but it is still attractive. They are also self-fertile so if you have a tiny, shady garden this is the tree for you.

There are three main mulberries; black, white and red. Unless you want to try for silk, the white mulberry is best avoided as it is inclined to grow into a slightly boring upright shape and the fruits tend to be tasteless. Red mulberries form attractive trees but are usually grown for their looks rather than their fruits. The black mulberry is a wonderful tree with amazing fruit. They frequently lean to one side and develop an aged appearance very rapidly. Within a matter of years you will have a tree which will look as if it has grown in your garden for many centuries. Their spreading branches eventually need support to prevent them collapsing onto the ground, but the forked wooden stakes traditionally used for this simply add to the charm of the tree. Like all fruit trees they lose their leaves in winter, but you are left with a striking skeleton of twisty branches. They need a sunny, sheltered site but are more tolerant of pollution than other fruits. Grow them in the middle of a lawn where they can be seen to their best advantage; the fallen fruit will be easy to gather and the purple juice will do no harm. As the fruits ripen and fall any surrounding paving will be stained a messy purple, as will you if you sit too long under the tree.

All cherries need vernalization or a period of winter chill, frost-free springs and reasonably warm summers. They will grow pretty well anywhere in Britain. In America sour cherries tend to do best east of the Rocky Mountains (USDA zones 4-8), especially in Michigan and New York, while to the west of the mountains sweet cherries predominate, centred in Washington, Oregon, Utah and California (USDA zones 5-9). Black mulberries will grow best in the warmer south of Britain and USDA zones 7-10.

Unless otherwise specified, the information in this chapter refers to both cherries and mulberries. We have used 'fruit trees' to mean these two fruits, although much of the advice would also be applicable to other orchard fruits such as apples, pears or plums.

FRUIT TREES IN THE GARDEN

Obviously you cannot have a large orchard of tall trees if you have a small patio garden in a city, but it is possible to grow cherries and mulberries in a small space, even on a balcony, although a window box might be pushing it. Most people imagine fruit trees as part of a large orchard but this is not the only option.

WITHIN A FLOWER GARDEN

In traditional cottage gardens there would often have been no room for an orchard, so the fruit was grown amongst the flowers (and vegetables). Whether your garden is large or small, cherries make good focal points in a flower bed, giving it height, and they usually crop well as they have the same need for sun, shelter and well-drained soil as most garden flowers. If you choose bee- and insect-friendly flowers they will also help with pollination.

You want fairly small trees in these situations but it is important that they start to branch out well above the tallest flowers. Trees on semi-dwarfing rootstocks usually work well. Mulberries tend to cast too dense a shade for much to grow well beneath them. It also pays to have a clear space round the base of a mulberry so you can easily collect the fruit as it falls.

You can use trained fruit to divide your garden, or as a backdrop to long borders. Espaliers can be supported on posts and wires while the trees are establishing their framework. Once this is established you can remove the supports leaving a flat fruiting sculpture. Fans will always need a framework but much of it will be covered by the spray of branches. This type of divide is very useful as it takes up much less room than a hedge whilst also being very beautiful.

Fruit trees have long seasons of interest; blossom and fruit are the obvious features but many have spectacular autumn colour and, depending on your tree, an interesting sculptural shape in winter. You can cut blossom for decoration, eat the fruit and use the wood for aromatic fires in winter. The beauty of the tree can be extended by growing climbers through the branches. The important thing is to balance the vigour of the climber to the size of the tree, so that the two are complimentary. Scottish flame flower, sweet peas and morning glory work well trained through smaller trees, and larger trees can support clematis and roses. Spring bulbs and lily of the valley look amazing beneath the blossom, and in summer shade-tolerant flowers such as alchemillas, aquilegias and hardy geraniums will do well beneath cherries.

In new gardens, fruit trees are useful as they grow reasonably quickly and give an instant sense of history to a garden. They make good specimen plants, whether at the centre of a sweeping lawn or in a small courtyard. Mulberries are traditional lawn centrepieces but also look lovely in a courtyard with paving beneath (as long as you don't mind the paving stones being stained purple). 'If I wanted the character of an oak in a small garden it would be a black mulberry every time. Where an oak might win on points with the amount of wildlife it would attract, a *Morus nigra* would win hands down in terms of its fruit. Acorns are good for pigs. Mulberries are very definitely the choice of humans.' So wrote gardener Dan Pearson in *Natural Selection*, and we tend to agree with him.

Kitchen Gardens

Free-standing cherries in a kitchen garden are a good way to grow fruit and the trees give height and permanent structure to what can otherwise be a rather flat part of the garden. Peas and beans can give temporary height, but a tree will be there throughout the year. Cherries are especially good partners for herbs. The herbs will attract pollinators and as herbs are usually cut rather than pulled up in the manner of annuals and many vegetables, the trees will not suffer root disturbance. Mulberries are perfect to place at the junction of paths.

Orchards

If you have room for four medium-sized trees, we think you are justified in calling it an orchard. The most important thing here is not to overcrowd your trees. You should give them space to grow as individuals, rather than a single mass; this will keep the trees healthier, give you more fruit and look better. If you don't have room for a traditional orchard you can create much the same feel with a grove of fruit trees; a path lined with spring bulbs and cherry trees will lift any heart.

If you can, it is best to mix old and young trees, although this is obviously dependent on there being some trees in place when you plant your orchard. If you are renovating an old orchard or adding to some existing trees, always leave some of the old trees in place, even if they are not particularly productive. In a small orchard there is no particular merit in aiming at uniformity, which is only really effective on a grand scale. Trees of different ages will add interest and it won't matter if a tree does weaken and needs replacing. Other fruit trees can, of course, be mixed in with your cherries and mulberries.

The grass is best left slightly longer than lawn grass and will create a lush green carpet. Somewhere to sit and picnic is vital, either on rugs beneath the trees or seats in between. Remember that the trees may spread their branches lower down the trunk and benches or seats should be placed alongside the trees rather than beneath them. Hens or ducks are a charming addition to small orchards, as are wild flowers with mown paths in between. It is worth adding some lighting; moonlit suppers are delightful, but it helps if you can see what you are eating. Well-positioned lights will also emphasize the shape of the trees but remember you want to cast gentle shadows, not recreate Blackpool.

LARGE ORCHARDS

Over the years orchards have changed, both in looks and use. To an Elizabethan it would have been a pleasure garden; somewhere to walk or sit that was both beautiful and productive. An early twentieth-century farmer's cherry orchard would have had tall trees with livestock grazing beneath. Nowadays most large or commercial orchards consist of symmetrical rows of low trees which are easy to pick. An orchard may have a few mixed trees or many hundreds of the same. Unless you are growing fruit purely for commercial reasons an orchard must surely also be somewhere to sit, picnic and play.

The spaces between the trees will depend on the varieties and rootstocks you have chosen. Equally spaced trees of a similar size will give your orchard a uniform feel, but there is no particular need for this approach. Larger trees surrounded by groups of smaller ones will give you a number of different areas of interest within the orchard. You can even create a maze of paths within the trees leading to an open centre with a special tree such as a mulberry. As long as you leave enough space between the trees it will be just as easy to harvest the fruit whether the varieties are all together or spread around the area. Do keep an accurate plan of which trees you plant where, as they can be surprisingly hard to identify once they have grown up and lost their nursery labels.

Animals grazing beneath tall trees will give a lovely old-fashioned feel to your orchard, but remember you will need to look after the animals as well as the orchard. Sheep or cows will keep the grass short and fertilize the soil. Pigs were also a common choice, with the Gloucester Old Spot often being referred to as the 'Orchard Pig'. You will need to protect young trees; cows may eat the leaves if they can reach them and any animal may damage the trees by rubbing up against them. Hens, ducks and geese will earn their keep by eating the insects and giving you eggs. Ducks do not scratch as much as chickens and therefore do less damage, but will need a pond to be truly happy. Geese are noisy and make brilliant guard dogs but this may not be what you want in an orchard. They are also most likely to damage young trees.

The prettiest orchards are set in a sea of wild flowers. Bulbs such as snowdrops, fritillaries, bluebells and scilla will provide a pretty carpet beneath the blossom, and daffodils look lovely in clumps around the trunks. Traditional meadow flowers such as poppies, campion, cornflowers and cranesbill geraniums then follow, lasting throughout the summer. The flowers will encourage beneficial insects and especially bees that will, in turn, help with pollination. At first it can be quite hard to achieve the correct balance of flowers and grasses in a meadow, but once you have got this right, looking after a meadow is easy, as you only have to cut it once a year in late summer or early autumn. Given this approach, your orchard will become a wildlife haven; birds, butterflies, bats and small mammals will all visit and settle. Bat and bird boxes can be attached to the trees and if you have mixed hedges round the edges they will provide even more habitats.

Bees are another worthwhile addition to an orchard, living in beautiful hives, pollinating the trees and providing you with honey. They are particularly easy to keep in a large orchard as you can position them in a relatively undisturbed area.

Containers

It is perfectly possible to grow cherries and mulberries successfully in containers. Naturally small cherries on dwarfing rootstocks ('Garden Bing' or 'Cinderella') and the recently-introduced mulberry bush (*M. rotundiloba* 'Charlotte Russe' ('Matsunaga') see page 72) allow you to have a harvest in the smallest of spaces. As long as your container is large enough and you don't disturb the roots you can also grow flowers and herbs around the base.

The final pot should be at least 45-60 cm / 18-24 inches wide and deep. Make sure it has holes in the base to allow water to escape and put crocks in the bottom with a layer of grit or gravel to help drainage. Use specialist compost (John Innes No 3 is good) or a soil-based multi-purpose compost with a third grit, perlite or sand added to open it up. You can also add moisture-retaining gel. If you buy a container-grown tree, do not put it straight into the large pot but gradually increase the size over a number of years. This will encourage the tree to grow slowly. Once the tree is in its final container it should be repotted every few years. Wait till the leaves have dropped, prune the roots if necessary and replace one third of the compost.

Regular maintenance is the most important thing for all container plants, especially constant supplies of water and nutrients. Never let them dry out in summer or become soggy in winter, and feed regularly, a high potassium liquid tomato food every fortnight during the growing season is ideal. (See below for general care and pruning.) Remember if you grow flowers or herbs in the same container you will need to provide proportionately more food and water. In cold weather, lag the pot to prevent the compost freezing.

CHOOSING AND CARING FOR YOUR TREES

Before planting or even choosing fruit trees you need to take stock of the space and conditions in your garden. A garden will not be a success if you do not take into account its climate, soil and aspect. Working within your natural constraints will always be more successful than trying to fight them. Cherries and mulberries are not hard to look after; all they require is a suitable site, sufficient space to spread their branches, some attention while young and a little routine care afterwards, mostly for the benefit of the harvester rather than the tree.

A Brief Note on Latin Names

Latin names may seem like a minefield to the unwary but it is worth getting to grips with the system as it will allow you to be certain exactly which tree you are buying. All plants are divided into families but these do not really have much impact on the gardener as they are divided botanically, not horticulturally. Slightly confusingly, cherries are part of Rosaceae, the rose family (see what we mean about families not helping gardeners?) while mulberries are in Moraceae, a much smaller family which also includes figs.

The genus is the next classification and here there are more pitfalls; sweet, sour and ornamental cherries all belong to the genus *Prunus* but, crucially, not all *Prunus* are cherries. Most *Morus* are mulberries but you will need to know the species to tell whether your tree will provide you with silk or berries. Once it is clear what you are referring to, the genus (the first word) can be abbreviated to a capital letter with a full stop (*P. cerasus*).

The 'species' is the second part of every plant's Latin name. The two parts of the name are always written in italics, with the first word starting with a capital letter (*Prunus avium*). It is this part of the name that will tell you whether you are buying a sweet cherry (*P. avium*), a sour one (*P. cerasus*) an almond (*P. dulcis*), a plum (*P. domestica*), a peach (*P. persica*) or a blackthorn (*P. spinosa*). There are black mulberries (*Morus nigra*), white mulberries (*M. alba*) and red mulberries (*M. rubra*). The species part of the name will often tell you more about the particular plant: *avium* meaning 'of the birds', even though we might like to think of the fruit as ours. *Nigra, alba* and *rubra* denote the colours black, white and red.

Cultivars are the next division you are likely to meet. These are cultivated varieties that differ horticulturally but not botanically and are often produced by the intervention of man. Confusingly they are often, incorrectly, called varieties. These are written in ordinary type, have capitals and quotation marks (*P. cerasus* 'Morello'). They are often proper names, commemorating the breeder's family and friends or famous people connected to the plant (*M. nigra* 'King James'). You may find plant labels saying something like 'Sweet cherry Stella'. Strictly speaking this is incorrect, but at least it is clear what you are buying. There are further subdivisions but you are unlikely to meet them buying fruit trees.

Fruit trees for sale are sometimes simply labelled by their common name, but it is worth seeking out different cultivars as it is here that you get the refinements, such as early or late harvests, particularly tasty fruits or compact plants. Heritage plants have historical interest and can be worth growing, but beware as they may be less productive or more disease-prone than more recent cultivars. Plants are increasingly bred with in-built resistance to pests and diseases, and these will make your gardening easier and your plants healthier.

The Site and Soil

Most of northern Europe and North America have perfect climates for growing fruit trees. In northerly or exposed areas or high altitudes you may need the protection of a wall. Note that it needs to be a wall to provide the extra warmth; wooden fences do not retain heat in the same way. All cherries flower early and are susceptible to frost damage, so avoid exposed sites or frost hollows. Sweet cherries are best in full sun whilst sour ones will also thrive in shade, doing particularly well trained against a shady wall. Mulberries like sun and an open position with a well-drained but moisture-retentive soil. Unless you have the perfect moist, well-drained, fertile soil that we would all like, it is worth adding organic matter to the soil before you plant. If your soil is very sandy this will also improve its structure, making it better able to hold nutrients. If you are planting in heavy clay you should also dig in sand or grit to improve the drainage. A pH of 6.5-7 is ideal but these trees are not particularly fussy. On a large scale it may be worth installing drainage and irrigation systems. Cherries in particular do not like their roots to be waterlogged and are more susceptible to disease if the soil is too wet, but they and mulberries both need a regular supply of water while the fruit is growing.

Pollination

To produce fruit, the flowers need to be pollinated. This means pollen must be transferred, by bees, insects or the wind, from the anther or male part of the flowers to the stigma or female part. Some cherries are self-fertile, meaning the flowers on a single tree are able to pollinate themselves, while others are self-sterile (self-infertile) and need to be planted near a suitable cultivar. Some are partially self-fertile which means that a single tree will produce fruit but that you will be assured a better harvest with a second, compatible tree. Any suitable tree within a clear 18 m / 60 feet will count, so those in neighbouring gardens may help. Cherries are divided into pollination groups based on flowering times and trees from neighbouring groups will pollinate each other. There is a pitfall though, as some cherries which flower at the same time are incompatible as pollinators. Many self-fertile cherries are universal pollinators, meaning they will pollinate any tree in the same or adjacent groups. The safest way to ensure adequate pollination is to buy your trees from a specialist nursery and ask their advice. Most cultivated mulberries are self-fertile, which means you only need a single tree.

Rootstocks

Cherries naturally grow into large trees and are usually sold as grafted plants; two compatible parts grafted or joined together, one above ground and one below. The rootstock, the below-ground portion, will determine the tree's final size, depending slightly on how vigorous the cultivar is and local conditions such as soil and aspect. It may also influence disease resistance and hardiness. The top or tree part will determine the fruit you get. Always check the rootstock and if the garden centre or nursery can't tell you, don't buy the tree. Everyone knows what a full size tree looks like, but when you get to semi-vigorous or semi-dwarfing different people have different ideas as to the exact size, whereas the rootstock provides a firm guide. The importance of this is that, within reason, you can have both the cultivar and size of tree of your choice. Thus you can have a fruit tree regardless of how little space you have.

As a general rule the more dwarfing the rootstock, the more care the plant will need throughout its life in terms of nutrition, watering and weeding. Small rootstocks need very good soil but in return they will flower and fruit a year or so earlier. Most trees will fruit within three or four years, though very vigorous rootstocks may take six or seven years, whereas very dwarf trees will begin in their second or third year. Below are the main cherry rootstocks available. The sizes refer to a fully-grown, freestanding tree.

F12-1 is a vigorous rootstock producing trees 7.5-10 m / 25-30 feet tall.

Mazzard not to be confused with mazzard trees, this rootstock is primarily available in America. F12-1 is a selection of it.

Colt is a semi-vigorous rootstock. Most trees will reach a maximum of 4.5 m / 15 feet in height and width. It is suitable for open trees, pyramids and large fans which will reach 5-5.5 m / 15-18 feet wide and 2.5 m / 8 feet tall.

Gisela 6 can be hard to find and produces trees in between Colt and Gisela 5.

Gisela 5 is a semi-dwarfing or dwarfing rootstock. The trees reach a maximum of about 3 m / 10 feet, making them perfect for most gardens. It can also be used for minarettes and smaller fans reaching 3.6 m / 12 feet wide and 2 m / 6 feet tall.

Gisela 3 is a recent rootstock which is more dwarfing.

You may also find **G.M.9, Damil** and **Tabel** which are all dwarfing.

Different rootstocks are especially suited for particular shapes of tree. Fans need to be grown on Gisela 5 or Colt so they can form the framework. Containers are best with Gisela 5, the container will restrict the size anyway and these rootstocks are better able to cope with the stresses of growing in a pot.

Mulberries are sold on their own rootstocks and grow into trees 10 m / 30 feet tall although they become twisted and gnarled, often appearing shorter and older than they actually are. Recently mulberry bushes have become available which have been bred from red and white mulberry crosses and these are perfect for containers.

Buying Plants

A fruit tree will be around for a long time so it is worth buying it from a specialist nursery or garden centre you really trust. The tree should be a good balanced shape and appear healthy, with leaves or buds according to the season. Check the graft looks firm with no cracking round the join and that it is above the level of the soil.

In a large garden, a sea of blossom looks amazing, but if you only have room for a few trees try to stagger the flowering times so you have a longer season of interest. To avoid the use of sprays, try to choose disease-resistant varieties.

Young trees will settle in more quickly and be better in the long run. For the first year after grafting a tree is called a maiden or whip and will have no side shoots. At two years the tree is called a feathered maiden and will have the beginnings of side branches (feathers) forming. Three years old is about the maximum age you should buy, as many trees start to flower and fruit in their fourth year and should be settled by then. If you want cherries in trained shapes it is best to buy trees which have been formatively pruned to point their branches in the right directions. Cherries do not take kindly to hard pruning so it is quite difficult to alter the basic shape of a tree.

Whether you buy bare-rooted or containerized plants doesn't really matter and will probably depend on your supplier. Just remember bare-rooted trees need to go into the ground immediately whereas plants in containers won't mind waiting a few days.

Spacing and Planting

The spacings between your trees will depend on the rootstock and how you want to train the plant. As a general rule the branches of different trees should not touch once they are fully grown. Work out the final spread of the trees and allow a few feet extra between each one. Minarettes should be planted at least 60 cm / 2 feet apart. This amount of space means the air circulates better and your trees will be healthier. It also looks better.

Cherries can be planted in late autumn or early winter. This ensures the soil is not too cold and gives the plant time to settle in before it has to worry about putting on new growth in the spring. Do not plant a fruit tree in exactly the same place as a previous one. Mulberries are best planted in early spring. They have brittle roots so need to be handled gently.

Choose a day when the soil is not waterlogged or frozen. Dig a hole large enough to accommodate the roots when they are spread out. If the soil is very compacted, break it up. Fix a stake so it will be on the windward side of the trunk. Containerized plants need an angled stake so you do not disturb the root ball. It should form an angle of 45 degrees to the ground on the windward side of the plant.

The plant will slowly develop its own mycorrhizae, but by adding some at the beginning you will give the plant a hugely increased chance of settling in and thriving. Always follow the instructions on the packet. Settle the tree in, double-checking that the graft union is above ground level. Firm in and water well. Fix the tree to the stake using tree ties or soft twine which will not damage the tree as it grows. You should then mulch with organic matter leaving a gap around the trunk to stop it rotting. This will stop weeds growing, conserve water and feed the tree.

MAINTENANCE

For the first three to four years all fruit trees will benefit from a little tender loving care. You should water the trees regularly to ensure they don't dry out, and feed and mulch them in the spring. Check the ties every few months to ensure they are not getting too tight. Stakes can usually be removed after two years. Shake the tree gently to check if the roots are firm. Always remove stakes at the start of the growing season to give the tree time to adjust while the weather is mild. Hard as it may seem, you should remove the blossom the first spring after planting, so the tree can concentrate on settling into its new home. For the same reason the area around the trunk should be kept clear of grass and weeds for the first couple of years. Trees on dwarfing rootstocks will always need a clear area, roughly equal to the diameter of the canopy.

All fruit trees will benefit from being mulched with well-rotted organic matter in spring and autumn. If the crop is poor one year, you can add a slow-release potash fertilizer in autumn. Always follow the instructions; too much is as harmful as too little. When the weather is dry, give each tree a bucket of water every day during the early stages of fruit production. It is important to keep the moisture levels reasonably constant while the cherries ripen to stop the skins splitting. Mulberries are thirsty trees and need water regularly during the growing season.

Frost is the cherry's main enemy (mulberries being too 'wise' to be caught like this). Horticultural fleece draped over a flowering plant should protect it from all but the worst of the late frosts. Make sure that the fleece doesn't rest on the blossom as it will still get frosted. Remove it gradually during the day to allow the plant to warm up slowly.

Neither cherries nor mulberries need thinning in the way that apples do.

The need for long ladders made harvesting or 'cherry-picking' a precarious job. As trees are now less tall, it is comparatively simple. Collect your cherries on a dry day as they will keep better and, particularly with sour cherries, cut rather than pull the stalks as this will prevent damage to the stem and next year's crop. Mulberries fall when they are ripe and the traditional method of harvesting was to spread a sheet beneath the tree to catch the fruit. When harvesting, be wary of the fact that the berries are extremely juicy and will stain anything they come into contact with, including the soles of your shoes and probably anything you subsequently walk on.

Pests and Diseases

Fruit trees are prone to a variety of diseases but many can be avoided by choosing resistant varieties and keeping your trees healthy. Ensure there is good air circulation and always remove any diseased or damaged branches. Make sure the soil drains well, especially in winter, and clear away fallen leaves. Vigorous, healthy trees will be able to fight off most problems. Creating a diversity of plants, both within the fruits and around them, will add to the general health of the garden.

Certain plants may help: garlic, chives, alliums, tansy and nasturtiums will all deter pests. Using chemicals will upset the natural balance of your orchard, may harm wildlife, and seems ludicrous when you are going to eat the crop. Many problems look much worse than they are and will not seriously harm your fruit. Mulberries in particular are fairly trouble-free.

Aphids / cherry blackfly: These may appear on the new shoots in early summer. On a small tree you can squash them by hand. As with most pests and diseases, prevention is the best method and a strongly-growing tree should be able to withstand a few aphids.

Birds: They can be a pest and will strip a cherry tree alarmingly quickly. In the days of huge trees, it was impossible to protect the crop. With the development of rootstocks which produce small trees, this need not be such a problem. If you have small or trained cherries it may be worth netting them, but bear in mind that you will need to set up the netting before the fruits start to colour and ensure that it does not rest on the fruits, allowing the birds to eat through the mesh. Otherwise it is probably worth losing a few fruits in return for birdsong in your garden and trees which are not swathed in nets. Birds tend to be less attracted to yellow cherries and do not usually bother with mulberries.

Blossom wilt: The blossom withers and rots. Prune back to a healthy joint.

Canker: This can affect all tree fruits, appearing as a gum which oozes from the trunk and branches, causing the leaves to turn yellow and fall. It is worst on poor, badly-drained soil so make sure your soil is in tip-top condition, adding lots of grit if necessary and topping up with a nutritious mulch in spring and autumn. For cherries only, prune on dry days in summer; for mulberries prune back as soon as any canker is noticed. Remove all the cuttings and burn or bag up.

Silver leaf: This can largely be avoided by only pruning cherries in summer when the spores are dormant and the tree's sap is rising.

Split fruits: Ensuring a regular supply of water while the cherries are growing will minimize this problem. It may occur during wet weather at harvest time. You obviously can't stand over the trees with an umbrella, but regular picking can avoid the problem.

Pruning

For free-standing trees, once developed, all you need to do is cut off the 'Three D's' (dead, diseased and damaged branches) and ensure that as much light and air as possible reaches all parts of the tree by removing crossing or inward-growing branches. The whole business of pruning may seem complicated, but in reality most trees will still crop without being pruned at all.

Cherries should be pruned as little as possible and only on a dry day in summer to reduce the risk of the serious disease silver leaf. The spores are dormant in summer and the rising sap of the tree will make it more resistant. Ideally sterilize your secateurs between each tree. Carry out the formative pruning of young trees in late spring. For an ordinary free-standing tree, you should cut the central leader just above the tallest side shoot. This will encourage the tree to develop into a good rounded shape rather than becoming tall and leggy. You should also cut the tips of the side shoots to encourage them to branch out. After three to four years the basic framework of the tree should be established.

General pruning should then be carried out immediately after harvesting. Sweet cherries fruit at the base of one-year-old stems and older stems, so you should only remove the 'Three D's' and any crossing branches. Sour cherries fruit along the length of one-year-old stems so, in addition, you should remove some of the older branches as they become less productive. Cut so the tree retains a balanced shape with new growth filling any gaps you create.

Mature mulberries need little pruning. They bleed sap from pruning cuts so any work should be carried out in early winter when the tree is dormant. While the trees are young cut back the leader and remove any low side shoots. As the tree gets older its branches will sag and fill this space. Diseased and damaged branches should be removed. You are likely to have to support your tree as it gets older; stout wooden posts at an angle to the tree look attractive and do the job. Check the angle of the branches regularly and support any that look as if they might need it; once the branch falls to the ground and breaks it is too late.

TRAINED FRUIT TREES

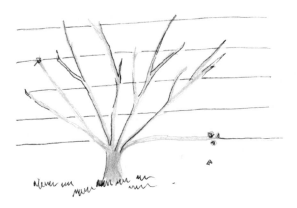

This is a useful and beautiful way of growing fruit in a restricted space. It will also extend the area you can grow fruit, as the tree will have extra protection in terms of warmth and shelter provided by the supporting wall (note that for warmth it needs to be a wall, not a fence as brick retains heat whereas wood does not). Cherries can be trained as fans or pyramids, mulberries usually look best as freestanding trees, although it is possible to train them as espaliers. To train cherries and mulberries it is best to buy a plant that has already been formatively trained into the right shape. The nursery should give you specific advice regarding subsequent training. Like all strictly trained or modified plants they will need constant care and training if they are to remain healthy and look their best.

Espaliers: These consist of a single central trunk with branches growing out horizontally at regular intervals. These trees need support to start with but once the framework is established they can become freestanding, creating an open boundary within your garden. Trees like this are incredibly beautiful, almost becoming fruit bearing works of art rather than mere trees. Mulberries can be trained as espaliers reaching 4.5 m / 15 feet wide and 2.5 m / 8 feet tall.

Fans: These are self-explanatory, with branches radiating outwards from a single central stem. They are not usually as sturdy as espaliers but they provide the most efficient coverage of a wall, with branches and fruit filling every inch of space. Fans suit cherries as their branches naturally sweep upwards. The final size will depend on the rootstock.

Pyramids: These are freestanding trees with a wide circular base rising to a conical point, which suits cherries. They are best grown up to 2.5 m / 8 feet and are a practical shape as well as being pretty, as the maximum light reaches all the branches.

Minarettes: Cherries can be grown as minarettes – a single vertical stem. They need constant pruning to prevent too much vertical growth at the expense of the productive side shoots, but are useful in a small space.

Propagation

It is, of course, possible to propagate your own trees. The problem is that as cherries do not come true from seed, you could plant a seed from a wonderfully compact and sweet-fruiting tree only to find that it grows into an unruly monster producing an unpalatable crop. Mulberries can be propagated by growing seeds but this will involve a fairly lengthy wait. Cuttings are a quicker option: in winter take a 25 cm / 10 inch piece of new growth with a heel and put it in a pot of multi-purpose compost with some vermiculite added. Keep moist and repot once new growth appears the following year. When the branches of old trees collapse onto the ground they frequently take root and a 10 cm / 4 inch thick branch, trimmed and hammered into the ground, will apparently also take root.

A SELECTION OF EDIBLE CHERRIES

Any fruit tree will rapidly become an important feature in your garden so it is worth choosing carefully. Most will outlive you and probably your children. There are now estimated to be nine hundred varieties of sweet cherries and three hundred of sour worldwide. Up until the 1960s the three main cultivars in Britain were 'Early Rivers', 'Napoleon Bigarreau' and 'Waterloo'. Most orchards in Victorian times were heavily sprayed against pests and diseases, and many of these varieties may not do so well if organically grown. Cultivars with the Royal Horticultural Society's Award of Garden Merit (AGM) are always reliable choices. Canada was responsible for the early self-fertile varieties 'Stella' and 'Sunburst', allowing gardeners to grow single productive trees.

WILD CHERRIES, GEANS AND MAZZARDS (*P. avium*)

Wild European cherries grow all over western and central Europe. They are known to have been eaten by the prehistoric lake-dwellers of Switzerland and are probably the ancestor of our present sweet cherry. The word gean comes from the Old French *guine* meaning sweet cherry. The trees usually grow at the edges of woodland, where they benefit from the sun and can reach up to 20 m / 70 feet. The fruits are small and sour but perfectly edible and can be used to flavour cherry brandy. They are much loved by birds, earning the plant its species name *avium*. The trees have red-banded bark, white blossom in spring, and in autumn the leaves turn attractive shades of red and orange. The name mazzard probably comes from the Anglo-Saxon 'maser' or bowl, referring to the shape of the flowers. It now tends to refer to cherries that are commonly grown in Devon and Cornwall, where the damper climate suits them better than the drier east of England.

P. a. '**Plena**' (double white cherry): This has fluffy double flowers and the same fruits and red autumn colour as its parent. It grows into a slightly smaller tree, reaching 12 x 12 m / 40 x 40 feet.

Sweet Cherries (*P. avium*)

These are sometimes divided into heart-shaped, which are shaped as you would expect with soft flesh and Bigarreaus which are rounded with firmer flesh.

'**Bing**': This was developed in Oregon and has dark red fruits. It is self-sterile. 'Garden Bing' is similar but smaller and self-fertile and can be grown in containers.

'**Kirstin**': This is the hardiest sweet cherry, it has nearly black fruit which ripens mid summer but is self-sterile.

'**Lapins**': This originated in Canada and is sometimes called 'Cherokee'. It has dark red, juicy fruits which are very sweet. Self-fertile, it is also a universal pollinator and has some resistance to canker and splitting.

'**Merton Glory**': The fruits are large, early and an attractive yellowy pink. It is resistant to canker but it is self-sterile and can be susceptible to splitting.

'**Napoleon Bigarreau**': This is an old cultivar dating back to the 1830s and was one of the cultivars traditionally grown in Kent in the early twentieth century. They are also called 'Naps' or 'Kentish Naps'. The large pale reddish-yellow fruits are firm and sweet. It is self-sterile and can be at risk of canker if grown in poorly drained soil.

'**Penny**': This is a comparatively recent cultivar raised at East Malling in Kent. It bears good crops of dark red fruits. It grows into a fairly compact tree and is tolerant of damp conditions but is self-sterile.

'**Stella**': This originated in British Columbia in the 1960s and was the first self-fertile sweet cherry. It is still one of the best sweet cherries to grow. The fruits are dark, with a good flavour. The trees are vigorous and upright and do best in warmer areas. It is resistant to canker but can be prone to splitting.

'**Summer Sun**': This fruits reliably in late summer with sweet, dark cherries. It is tolerant of colder and exposed sites, has some resistance to canker, and is partially self-fertile although it will produce more fruit with a compatible pollinator.

'**Sunburst**': This is another self-fertile cherry from Canada which can also be used as a universal pollinator. The fruits are large, almost black and very sweet, but can be prone to splitting.

'**Sweetheart**': This is a self-fertile cherry whose fruits ripen over a long period continuing into late summer after most other sweet cherries have finished. This gives you a regular supply of fruit rather than a glut.

Sour, Acid or Tart Cherries (*P. cerasus*)

These tend to be smaller trees than wild sweet cherries and are commonly found in hedgerows and open woodland in Britain, Europe and Central Asia. The trees usually flower later than sweet cherries and the fruits tend to ripen earlier. Cultivated sour cherries divide into morellos and amarelles. Morellos possibly came to western Europe via southern Spain, as the name morello may mean 'little Moor'. These are called *griottes* in France where they are widely used in confectionery and eau de vie. The fruits have bright red flesh and produce dark juice. The name amarelle possibly comes from the Italian word *marelle* meaning bitter, but confusingly they are also known as red morellos. They are more common in North America and are bright red with pale flesh and clear juice. Nearly all sour cherries are self-fertile and many will act as universal pollinators.

'**English Morello**': This grows into a naturally small tree with drooping branches that are easy to harvest from. The fruits ripen late and are less sour than most morellos.

'**Montmorency**': This is an amarelle with bright red fruits that ripen in early summer. This is the cultivar Nigel Slater recommends for the best jam.

'**Morello**': This is the best known and, in many ways, best cultivar. The fruits are bright red and are sharp without being too acidic. It is reliably self-fertile but will produce even better crops with a pollinator and will pollinate most late-flowering cherries. It is happy trained against a north- or east-facing wall and has good resistance to canker and splitting.

'**Nabella**': This originated in Germany. It crops well with deep red fruits and is resistant to splitting and canker.

'**Northstar**': This is a naturally dwarfing morello, rarely reaching more than 3 m / 10 feet. It bears deep red fruits and has good resistance to cold.

DUKES

Dukes are a hybrid of the sweet and sour cherries, with many of the best features of both. The fruits have good flavour with just a hint of acidity. The trees should be cultivated in the same way as sweet cherries and tend to be easier and healthier. If you are lucky the birds will largely ignore the fruits.

'**May Duke**': This is the cultivar you are most likely to find. The fruits ripen in mid season and are red and sweet with an edge of sharpness. They can be eaten fresh or used for cooking. Partially self-fertile, a single tree will produce fruit but will give a better crop with a compatible pollinator.

OTHER EDIBLE CHERRIES

A selection of less common cherries, some more edible than others.

Cornelian cherries (*Cornus mas*): These are not really cherries but dogwoods, though they earn their place here as they produce good tart fruits. They form shrubs or small trees, rarely reaching more than 5 m / 15 feet. Small yellow flowers appear in late winter before the leaves and the oval fruits, then ripen towards the end of summer turning bright red before the leaves turn purple and fall. This is a good all-round plant and although the fruits are usually too sour to eat fresh, they are great for cooking. The trees are partially self-fertile but will crop better with another cultivar.

Western sand cherry (*P. besseyi*): Native to the Great Plains of North America this shrub grows up to 2 m / 6 feet tall. Clouds of fragrant white blossom in late spring are followed by dark crimson cherries which can be bitter and are mostly used for cooking. It is a useful plant as it is tolerant of all soils, will cope with drought once established, and is largely pest- and disease-free. Plant two for pollination.

Maraschino cherries (*P. cerasus* var. *marasca*): These cherries are native to Dalmatia and are distilled to produce a cordial or liqueur in Italy. The fruits are dark red. The bright pinky-red maraschino cherries sold in jars are usually sweet cherries, dyed and soaked in almond-flavoured syrup.

Cherry laurel (*P. laurocerasus*): This is a common evergreen garden shrub which bears fragrant white flowers in spring and (poisonous) red fruits that ripen to black. It looks similar to the bay tree but has larger, glossier leaves. The French for bay is *laurier* which can lead to confusion. Cherry laurel leaves contain Prussic acid and, although their almond flavouring can be used in milky puddings, you are probably safer using almond extract.

St Lucie cherries (*P. mahaleb*): This is a spreading, deciduous tree reaching 10 m / 30 feet by 8 m / 25 feet. In mid to late spring there are clusters of bowl-shaped, very fragrant white flowers which are followed by ovoid glossy red cherries ripening to black, and rather beautiful yellow autumn colour. The fruits are edible but the trees are predominantly grown as ornamentals or for their timber, which was used for smokers' pipes and decorative walking sticks.

Black cherry, **Wild rum cherry** (*P. serotina*): This is a North American bird cherry and grows into a large tree reaching 35 m / 120 feet by 12-18 m / 40-60 feet. The scented white flowers form short spikes and are followed by red cherries which ripen to black. They were formerly used to flavour rum. The leaves turn attractive reds and yellows in autumn. The trees do not start producing fruit until they are about ten years old, but will then crop for about a hundred more. It was introduced into Europe in 1629 and was frequently grown for its timber.

Nanking cherries (*P. tomentosa*): This forms a rounded shrub 2-3 m / 6-10 feet tall. Pinky-white blossom is followed by bright red berries that are sweet with a hint of acidity. You need to plant at least two for pollination.

Pin cherry, Fire cherry or Pigeon cherry (*P. pensylvanica*) and the Barbados or West Indian cherry (*Malpighia punicifolia*) bear edible fruits, will grow in temperate regions and may be worth experimenting with.

Australian brush cherry (*Szygium* spp. syn. *Eugenia, Acmena, Waterhousea*), the Brazilian cherry and Surinam cherry (*Eugenia uniflora, E. michelii, Stenocalyx michelii*), the Capulin or Tropic cherry (*P. salicifolia*), the Cherry of the Rio Grande (*Eugenia aggregata*) and the Husk or Peruvian ground cherry, better known as the Cape gooseberry (*Physalis peruviana* syn. *P. edulis*), all bear edible fruits but require a warm climate.

A SELECTION OF MULBERRIES

There are a few named cultivars of black mulberries, but they are all fairly similar ('Black Persian', 'Black Beauty' and lots of other 'Black something-or-other'). Most will eventually reach 10 m / 30 feet although they may not appear this tall as their branches bend and dip towards the ground. Just be sure you buy a black mulberry (*Morus nigra*), not a white (*M. alba*) or red (*M. rubra*) one.

M. n. '**Giant Fruit**': This cultivar comes from Pakistan and bears large fruits, up to two or three times the size of others.

M. n. '**King James**' syn. '**Chelsea**': This is the cultivar reputed to be the descendent of the mulberries planted by King James I in the seventeenth century. True or not, the trees bear good fruit and are reliably problem-free. This is the cultivar you are most likely to find.

M. n. 'Illinois Everbearing': This American cultivar was discovered growing wild and may have been a cross between red and white mulberries. It grows into a large tree, crops over a long period and is tolerant of cooler climates.

M. rotundiloba 'Charlotte Russe' ('Matsunaga'): this is a hybrid which flowers on new and old wood and remains small enough to grow in a container. It is self-fertile, crops from summer to early autumn and reaches a height of 1.5 m / 5 feet.

OTHER MULBERRIES

Paper mulberries (*Broussonetia papyrifera*): These are distantly related to *Morus* mulberries and originated in northeast Asia. They grow into medium-sized trees (8 m / 25 feet height and width) and will thrive in tropical or temperate climates. The fruits are a brilliant orangey-red and ripen to sweet-tasting mulberry-like berries in autumn. The bark can also be used to make paper, cloth and rope.

Chinese mulberry, Silkworm thorn or **Che** (*Maclura tricuspidata* syn. *Cudriania tricuspidata*): These are fast-growing but comparatively short-lived deciduous trees (about thirty years), which are primarily used in China to feed silkworms if white mulberry leaves are unavailable. They are pretty trees, reaching about 7 m / 22 feet with tiny clusters of green flowers in summer, followed by glossy, edible orangey-red fruits. You need a female tree for the fruits.

ORNAMENTAL CHERRIES

Looking up through the branches at blue sky hustled with clouds and the first petals drifting to the ground.

(Monty Don, *The Ivington Diaries*)

As the weather starts to warm in early spring, the princess Ko-no-hana-sakuya-hime ('the maiden who causes trees to bloom' in Japanese mythology, the goddess of flowers and volcanoes, including Mount Fuji), breathes gently on the trees to awaken them from their winter sleep. There may be many more prosaic reasons for the trees to bloom but this is surely the most charming.

Many cherry trees are grown purely for their spectacular spring blossom. All fruiting cherries have lovely blossom, but ornamental varieties will give you a much greater range of colour, shape and flowering time. The extra petals that many of them have come at the expense of the fruit, although the fruits which follow are often edible and always loved by birds. From a deep rosy pink to the purest white, these trees put on a spectacular display of single flowers, double flowers or fluffy pompoms, creating clouds of colour against the stark spring skies. Many also have brilliant autumn colours, but it is in spring that these trees really show off.

Cherry blossom festivals began in Japan, where there are now over a million ornamental cherry or *sakura* trees. Much of the symbolism surrounding them is linked to ancient Japanese beliefs based on Buddhism, the importance of the seasons and the natural world. At first the strength of the blossom was used to foretell the harvests and although this symbolism has shifted over the years to fit with modern ways of life, in essence it remains the same. The brief displays of flowers are linked with beginnings and endings, in particular our brief lives on earth. Like mankind, the flowers are perishable and only live for a short time. Their beauty shows that transience can be a good thing and that we should all try to live as purely as we can. As Japan's national flower the cherry blossom symbolizes the perfection towards which we should all strive. The flowers also came to be linked with women and the temporary pleasures of the company of geishas and courtesans. Some species of cherry tree have been used for memorials: *Prunus serrulata* was used as a symbol for those who died when the atom bombs were dropped on Hiroshima and Nagasaki in 1945.

At first, *hanami* or the custom of viewing cherry blossom was a pastime reserved for the emperor and the higher aristocracy of Japan. It began in the eighth century and, like many things in Japan at that time, was copied from the Chinese. In China, the plum blossom, which came in February, coincided with the start of the new lunar year and offered hope for the summer to come, despite the continuing snows. In Japan, the festival was transferred to cherry blossom, which flowered slightly later when the weather was warmer. In 834 AD Emperor Ninmei planted a cherry tree rather than a plum in front of the main hall of the Imperial Palace confirming the tree's pre-eminence. Viewing traditions and rituals were established and are described in *The Tale of Genji*, written in the early eleventh century by a noblewoman, Murasaki Shikibu, one of the court's ladies-in-waiting. The bulk of the novel describes the life and loves of Genji, son of the Emperor, and gives a fascinating insight into court life and rituals at the time. The Festival of the Cherry Blossoms is described with concerts, dancing and banquets. The princes and courtiers were also expected to compose poems, an activity which some enjoyed more than others. And, of course, all this merriment was the perfect backdrop for a little court intrigue and romance.

By the thirteenth century the festivals had expanded to include the Samurai. These men of war were highly disciplined and cultured, and their goal was to die an honourable death, ideally while still young and in the service of their overlord, a goal which was frequently likened to the blossom. From the early seventeenth century until the middle of the nineteenth, the Shoguns virtually controlled Japan, with the Samurai ruling below them. In effect, the Shoguns were military dictators, wielding far more power than the emperors in whose names they ruled. During this time the country had almost no contact with the outside world; foreigners were expelled, travel abroad was forbidden, ships could not be built over a certain size, and trade was restricted to a few Dutch merchants. The country looked in on itself, it was a time of repression but also one of stability, with tradition and social duties being some of the lynchpins of society. Festivals such as *hanami* were important and as more Japanese moved to the towns, the celebrations changed slightly. More people took part and picnics were held beneath the trees, with tea and sake being consumed in equal measure. Rather than having to recite poems, participants now wrote them on *tanzaku* or slips of paper which were attached to the trees. The poems could either be composed on the spot or copied beforehand, the idea being that the words would live on after the blossom had gone. Girls would wind a strand of their hair round a tree in full bloom as a love spell to entice the man of their dreams.

When Japan was opened to the western world in 1854 with the treaty of Kanagawa, visiting foreigners were mystified by the extraordinary country and its ideals. Cherry blossom viewing was one of the few things they could understand and blossom paintings, drawings and fabric were an important part of the craze for Japonism which swept much of Europe and America in the late nineteenth century.

In the twentieth century, blossom again became a poignant symbol for a short life lived well. In the 1904-05 Russo-Japanese War it was used on flags and became linked with the old Samurai belief of dying well in battle. Thirty years later Japan's young soldiers, and in particular the infamous kamikaze pilots, went eagerly to their deaths encouraged by propaganda to see themselves as flowers falling from the trees in the prime of their lives.

Nowadays *hanami* is no longer restricted to the Japanese aristocracy. Indicator trees are chosen in each area and once sufficient blooms are open, the official start of the cherry blossom season is announced, unleashing a mad commercial frenzy of everything pink. The entire country listens to the radio forecasts which tell exactly how far up the islands the cherry blossom front has reached, and on the appropriate day busloads of workers are taken to view the sight, picnicking beneath the flowers. Monitoring cherry blossom timings is considered every bit as important as monitoring storms and hurricanes. It creeps from south to north, beginning in the most southerly island of Okinawa in January, spreading up to reach Tokyo and Kyoto in mid April, and finally the most northerly island of Hokkaido in May. The old traditions of celebrating the arrival of spring, drinking tea or sake and writing poems to attach to the trees continue, but the festivals also now have a wider sense of beginnings, as April is the start of both the school and the financial year.

The spread of Japanese art and culture was mirrored by an expansion of their plants, and from the late nineteenth century onwards ornamental cherry trees were widely grown in Europe and North America. Our festivals obviously have some way to go to catch up on the Japanese ones, but in Britain there is a long tradition of celebrating the arrival of spring and A. E. Housman poignantly connected cherry blossom with the ephemeral nature of our existence in *A Shropshire Lad*:

Loveliest of trees, the cherry now
Is hung with bloom along the bough,
And stands about the woodland ride
Wearing white for Eastertide.

Now, of my threescore years and ten,
Twenty will not come again,
And take from seventy springs a score,
It only leaves me fifty more.

And since to look at things in bloom
Fifty springs are little room,
About the woodlands I will go
To see the cherry hung with snow.

In Britain, cherry blossom is also associated with hope and love, themes poignantly shown in H. E. Bates' short story 'The Wild Cherry Tree', where the purity of the tree in bloom stands in sharp contrast to the story's setting in a very grubby pig farm. The tree is the catalyst for a brief but moving love story between the wife of the pig farmer and a suitably enigmatic passing stranger.

At both Brogdale and Batsford Arboretum, *hanami* are held each spring. Brogdale, in Kent, has the world's largest collection of fruit trees, and as well as fields of fruiting cherries there is a plantation of ornamental cherries where you can picnic beneath the flowers and Japanese lanterns. Sake is an option but, given the unpredictability of English spring weather, a nice cup of hot tea is often more welcome. At Brogdale the trees are planted in neat rows as befits an orchard, but at the Batsford Arboretum in Gloucestershire they are placed in a Japanese setting, with a traditional bridge and tea house showing the national collection off beautifully. Keele University in Staffordshire also holds a national collection, and London parks and gardens all have fantastic displays in spring.

At Whipsnade forest park there is an extraordinary 'Tree Cathedral', with cherry and apple blossom trees, hedges and shrubs planted in the form of a medieval cathedral. In 1930 Captain Edmund Blyth visited Liverpool's Anglican Cathedral and was inspired to plant a living memorial to his companions who had died in the First World War. The 'Easter Chapel' consists entirely of cherry trees which lighten the countryside with their blooms each spring and bring to mind 'The Cherry Tree' by Edward Thomas, describing the same war:

The cherry trees bend over and are shedding,
On the old road where all that had passed are dead,
Their petals, strewing the grass as for a wedding
This early May morn when there is none to wed.

Of the many festivals in the United States the one held in Washington DC is probably the most renowned. In 1912 Japan gave the city over 3,000 trees and it is these that form the heart of the display. Three years earlier, the United States Department of State had received a letter from the City of Tokyo stating that they wished to make a gift as thanks for America's help in the treaty ending the Russo-Japanese War of 1904-05.

In the event the first 2,000 trees had to be destroyed due to fears regarding the spread of pests and diseases, but the 3,020 trees donated in 1912 flourished, with some still surviving today. The trees here do not have a particularly long lifespan as the parks are a surprisingly stressful environment for them. The constant passage of feet compacts the ground, forcing the trees' roots up nearer the surface to get the air they need. This makes them more vulnerable to cold, wet and drought and the trees do well to live over a hundred years. In their natural habitats in Japan they are more long-lived and there are trees reputed to be nearly two thousand years old.

The trees were an instant success and remained a popular meeting place even during the Second World War, when the two countries were on opposing sides. During this period they were called 'oriental cherry trees', but with the advent of peace friendly relations resumed

and in 1965 a further 3,800 trees were donated. Each year blossom festivals are held with picnics, parades and traditional Japanese displays. Cherry blossom festivals are now held in nearly all countries where the trees grow, often donated by local Japanese residents and businesses. China, Taiwan, Korea and the Philippines all have a long tradition of these parties. In Finland, 200 donated cherry trees were planted in Helsinki in Kirsikkapuisto ('Cherry Tree Park') where *hanami* is celebrated, and in Rome it is celebrated in the Eur Park where there are trees donated by Japan in 1959.

Growing Ornamental Cherry Trees

In *The Ivington Diaries* Monty Don movingly describes the cherry tree (*Prunus* 'Kanzan') in the garden where he grew up. After the age of seven he never saw it because he was away at boarding school, yet its impact has remained: 'I can clearly remember the thick pink puffiness of the tree in full blossom, the flowers exactly the colour of Wall's strawberry ice cream.' The important thing when choosing an ornamental cherry is to be sure you will be there to see it when it is in full bloom.

Japanese or flowering cherries were developed in East Asia as purely ornamental trees. Their blossom and autumn colours are often spectacular, but they rarely bear edible fruit. There are many closely related flowering cherries; in Japan they are called village cherries and were originally grouped together as *P. serrulata* but are now usually referred to by their cultivar name. One of the most famous, 'Mikuruma Gaeshi' or 'The Royal Carriage Returns' cherry no longer exists, but is said to be the ancestor of all these cultivars. Tradition has it that many years ago a royal carriage passed this tree while it was in blossom and then returned, giving the plant its name. Some sources give the reason as courtiers arguing over whether the flowers were single or double, but we prefer the alternative explanation given, that the emperor was overcome by the beauty of the tree.

Another famous cherry was the 'Usuzumi-No-Sakura' tree which was declared a national treasure in Japan in 1922. It is believed that the 26th Emperor Keitai Tenno planted one of these trees fifteen hundred years ago to commemorate the eighteen years he lived in the village of Neo Mura in Gifu Prefecture, where the trees still grow. The flowers are pink tinged, then fading to white and finally grey before falling.

Blossom is categorized by colour, size, number of petals and flowering time. Most flowers range from pure white to deep pink, although green and yellow flowers can be found. The exact flowering time depends on the weather, with all trees within a cultivar flowering at the same time in an area. Cherries need 1,200 hours below 0° C / 32° F (vernalization) and most will come into flower when daytime temperatures are between 17-20° C / 65-70° F.

Some cherry trees blossom in winter, usually whenever there is a warm spell. In Andrew Lang's *The Violet Fairy Book* of 1901 there is a delightful explanation for this in 'The Envious Neighbour', a Japanese folk tale. The tale involves an elderly couple, their remarkably gifted dog and a greedy neighbour who comes to a satisfactorily sticky end. Following the dog's instructions, the old man causes cherry trees to come into bloom many months early, just as the feudal lord is passing. Stunned by the beauty of the trees the lord showers gifts on the old man. The more prosaic reason is that some species are simply adapted to flower earlier in the year.

Flowers may be single (a single layer of petals) or double (with two or more layers of up to thirty individual petals). Some flowers bloom before the leaves appear, creating beautiful cloud-like effects within the trees. In Japan different varieties are used for specific effects, with double-flowered trees planted singly at important places and single varieties planted in groups to provide a mass of blossom.

In terms of planting and care their requirements are similar to sweet cherries (see page 48). Allow space between each tree, even if you are planting an orchard, they prefer it and you will get a better view of the spring and autumn colours.

A Selection of Ornamental Cherries (*P.* spp.)

All the trees listed below are deciduous. They are hardy (USDA zone 6) unless specified otherwise and do not do well in tropical climates. Many of the plants below are given their common names (they are often too charming to ignore) but they are listed alphabetically by their Latin names to avoid confusion.

Flagpole cherry (*P.* 'Amanogawa'): This upright tree lacks the sweeping beauty of many cherries but is useful for small spaces. Its Japanese name means 'celestial river' and in late spring the saucer-shaped or semi-double pale pink fragrant flowers along the length of its branches fully justify this description. The yellowish-bronze leaves turn green and then red and yellow in autumn. 6-8 m / 20-25 feet tall by 3.6 m / 12 feet wide.

Gean (*P. avium*): These trees bear beautiful white flowers in late spring but they cast deep shade once in leaf and tend to send up a lot of suckers. This means it is hard to grow much beneath them and they are best suited to large gardens where you can admire their beauty from a distance.

***P. a.* 'Plena'** has larger flowers but is slightly less hardy (USDA zone 8). 12 m / 40 feet tall and 8 m / 25 feet wide.

Taiwan cherry (*P. campanulata*): The spreading trees bear open bowl-shaped pink or red flowers in early to mid spring, with or before the leaves, and are followed by cherry-like red fruits. 8 m / 25 feet tall and wide.

Fuji cherry (*P. incisa*): This is a spreading tree with pink buds which open into single white flowers, borne singly or in clusters of 2-3 before the leaves in early to mid spring. The leaves are bronze-red when young, turning a more orange shade in autumn. The flowers are followed by ovoid cherry-like purple-black fruits. 8 m / 25 feet height and width.

***P. i.* 'February Pink'** has pale pink flowers over a long period from winter to early spring.

***P. i.* 'Kojo-no-mai'** has light red buds which open to pale pink flowers, singly or in pairs. The leaves start off yellowy-green, maturing to mid green and then turning rusty-red in autumn. It is a slightly larger cultivar, with a height and width reaching 10 m / 30 feet.

***P. i.* 'Praecox'** has pink buds that open to white flowers in late winter.

***P.* 'Kanzan'** (often incorrectly written as *P.* 'Kwanzan'): The trees bear bright pink double flowers which hang in clusters from the branches. They have dark reddish-brown bark and grow into a vase shape, spreading with age and reaching up to 10 m / 30 feet in height and width. These trees are best viewed from below so you can look up through the deep pink pompoms of blossom. The reddish-green leaves begin to appear while the tree is still in flower and turn orange in autumn.

Manchurian cherry (*P. maackii*): The reddish-golden bark of these trees is their main feature and often peels away in large sheets. The fragrant white flowers are small but grow in dense clusters, the long stamens making them appear yellowish. They are followed by spherical, cherry-like glossy black fruit. These trees originate in northeast Asia and came to western Europe via St Petersburg in 1910. They are very hardy and will thrive in USDA zone 2 but will not do well in warmer areas above zone 7. They reach 10 m / 30 feet by 8 m / 25 feet, occasionally reaching 12 m / 40 feet tall.

P. 'Okame': This is one of the earliest cherries to flower. It is a hybrid between a Fuji cherry tree (*P. incisa*) and a Taiwan cherry (*P. campanulata*) and forms a bushy tree. There is a profusion of clusters of candyfloss pink flowers in early spring, followed by red and orange leaf colour in autumn. Its usual height is 10 m / 30 feet by 8 m / 25 feet. *P.* 'Dream Catcher' was developed in 1999 at the U. S. National Arboretum from the Okame cherry tree. The hope was to create a flowering cherry which would be resistant to disease and pests, tolerant of the wide climatic variations in America and, of course, beautiful. It is a tall, oval tree, reaching 8 m / 25 feet. The early pink single flowers are followed by dark green leaves which turn brilliant shades of red and orange in autumn.

P. 'First Lady': Following on from the development of *P.* 'Dream Catcher', this was introduced in 2003. It is a tall, narrow tree with a height of 8 m / 25 feet and width of 4.5 m / 14 feet. The semi-pendulous flowers bloom early and are deep carmine pink.

Bird cherry (*P. padus*): These trees are conical when young, gradually spreading with age. The fragrant white flowers grow in unusual spikes or racemes, giving the tree a resemblance to a rather dainty buddleia. The late spring blossom is followed by glossy pea-like black fruits which are quickly eaten by birds, earning the tree its name. The leaves turn red and yellow in autumn. They need full sun but will grow happily on poor soil. 15 m / 50 feet tall by 10 m / 30 feet wide.

P. p. 'Albertii' has very dense flowers.

P. p. 'Colorata' has pink flowers and reddish-purple young foliage.

P. p. 'Wateri' is a taller tree with long slender racemes.

Weeping cherries (*P. pendula* f. *ascendens* often written as *P.* x *subhirtella*, which is what they used to be.)

P. p. f. *a.* 'Pendula Rosea' has weeping branches which spread out so that the tree is often wider than its height of about 5 m / 16 feet with pale, rose pink blossom.

P. p. f. *a.* 'Pendula Rubra' is similar with deep pink blossom in early spring.

P. p. f. *a.* 'Stellata' was raised in California and is so called because its pale pink flowers have pointed petals and resemble little stars. It grows into a particularly dainty upright shape.

Sargent's cherry (*P. sargentii*): This tree originated in Japan and Korea but was widely distributed from America in 1890. It was named after Charles Sprague Sargent who was Director of the Arnold Arboretum, Massachusetts. In Japan it is often called the Great Mountain Cherry. It is a large tree and can reach 18 m / 60 feet tall by 15 m / 50 feet wide. It has smooth dark brown bark and single pink flowers in early to mid spring. The foliage is red when young, turning a brilliant orange-red in autumn. Unlike most ornamental cherries it regularly produces edible fruit. It is very hardy (USDA zones 4-7). 8 m / 25 feet tall by 12 m / 40 feet is an average size.

P. s. 'Columnaris' is narrow and upright, reaching 3 m / 10 feet wide.

P. s. 'Rancho' is similar.

Black cherry (*P. serotina*): Also called the rum cherry, this species is native to North America but also common in Europe. It has short spikes of white flowers followed by small reddish-black edible cherries. In autumn the leaves turn red and yellow. When young, the bark is smooth and banded but after about ten years it becomes dark grey, rough and scaly. It reaches 35 m / 120 feet tall and 12-18 m / 40-60 feet wide.

Tibetan cherry (*P. serrula*): The glossy coppery-red, peeling bark of these trees is more important than their blossom. The flowers are small and white, emerging in late spring and growing into pairs of little red fruits. The trees grow quickly and the main trunk often divides, creating a broad crown and which can reach up to 7-10 m / 23-30 feet tall and wide.

P. **'Shirofugen'**: These spreading trees have clusters of pink buds which open to double, fragrant white flowers. They bloom about two weeks later than Yoshino cherries extending the blossom time into summer. The leaves are bronze-red when young, turning orange-red in autumn. 8 m / 25 feet tall by 10 m / 30 feet wide.

Mount Fuji cherry (*P.* 'Shirotae'): This low spreading tree bears flowers the length of its branches which are said to resemble the snow in the gullies on Mount Fuji. The pure white semi-double flowers are one of the earliest to appear. 10 m / 30 feet tall and wide.

Higan cherry (*P.* x *subhirtella*): These trees bloom about a week before the Yoshinos, taking their name from *higan*, the Japanese for equinox, with which they often coincide. They are sometimes known as rosebud or spring cherries. There are also autumn flowering cherries within this group which have a second, lesser flowering during the warm weather around the time of the autumn equinox. Higan cherries vary widely in shape but the blossom usually appears before the leaves, creating delicate clouds of flowers. The leaves are bronze when young, maturing to dark green and finally fading to yellow in autumn. The blossom is sometimes followed by ovoid, cherry-like fruit, starting red, later turning nearly black. The trees are usually bowl-shaped reaching 8 m / 25 feet in height and width although they can grow up to 12 m / 40 feet tall. Many half-wild trees can be found in Japan where they are very long-lived, with some reputed to be over a thousand years old. There are a great many cultivars, all of which are very hardy (USDA zones 4-5). Their only problem is that they can be susceptible to fungal blossom wilt, especially when grown close together.

P. x *s.* **'Autumnalis'** has small clusters of semi-double, pink-tinged, white flowers which appear intermittently in mild periods between autumn and spring. It is very tolerant of soil and aspect, and never casts a deep shade. Its blossom is dainty rather than brash and it is a good tree for all but the smallest gardens.

P. x *s.* **'Autumnalis Rosea'** has red buds opening to pink flowers.

Great white cherry (*P.* 'Tai-haku'): The story behind this tree is as interesting as the tree is beautiful. In 1923 Captain Collingwood Ingram was shown a nameless white cherry tree in a Sussex garden. He thought the tree was attractive and took grafts. On his next visit to Japan he was shown an eighteenth-century book of flower paintings, one of which he recognized as the tree in Sussex. In Japan, the tree had been extinct for years; how it came to be in an English country garden no one knew. The tree bears clusters of spectacular bowl-shaped white flowers in spring in amongst coppery-red leaves. 8 m / 25 feet by 10 m / 30 feet height and width.

P. 'Ukon': The unusual feature of this cultivar is its blossom, which is yellow, *ukon* being Japanese for the colour. Clusters of pink buds open in mid spring to double flowers, yellowish-white on the outside and pinkish at the tips. The leaves are reddish-bronze when young, turning increasingly purply-brown towards autumn. It grows to 8 m / 26 feet x 10 m / 30 feet height and width.

P. 'Umineko': As well as rediscovering *P.* 'Tai-haku' Collingwood Ingram also bred this cultivar which is a cross between *P. incisa* and *P. speciosa*. It is ideal for small gardens as the branches sweep gracefully upwards and don't take up too much room, while still giving a spectacular display of pure white flowers. Its name means seagull, and when in flower the tree does indeed resemble a giant bird in flight.

Yoshino or **Somei-Yoshino Cherry** (*Prunus* x *yedoensis*): This species was originally cultivated in the Imperial Botanic Garden in Tokyo as a cross between *P. speciosa* and *P. subhirtella* 'Rosea', and was recognized in 1872. It is also called the 'Tokyo Cherry' as there are around 50,000 specimens growing in the city. It reached Europe in 1902 and America in 1912. These trees have a rounded, spreading shape and will grow up to 10 m / 30 feet in height and width. They bloom early and bear faintly almond-scented flowers which open from light pink buds, the flowers fading from pale pink to white. These are followed by small, shiny black fruits which are popular with birds.

P. x *y.* 'Akebono', also known as **'Daybreak'**, was named by W. B. Clarke of San Jose, California in 1920. The trees are slightly smaller than the species with flowers which open as a deeper pink and then fade to white.

P. x *y.* **'Afterglow'** are smaller again, reaching a height and width of 7.5 m / 24 feet. Unlike most other Yoshinos their flowers remain pink and do not fade.

P. x *y.* 'Shidare-Yoshino' syn. *P.* x *y.* 'Pendula' and *P.* x *y.* 'Perpendens' have weeping branches which arch down to the ground.

Places to View Cherry Blossom

Japan
Tokyo: Ueno Park, Shinjaku Gyoen Park, Edo Castle Moat
Osaka: Osaka Mint, Osaka Castle
Kyoto: Philosopher's Trail, Maruyama Park, Heian Shrine, Arashiyama
Nagoya: Nagoya Castle

UK
Brogdale, Brogdale Road, Faversham ME13 8XZ
Batsford Arboretum, Moreton-in-the-Marsh GL56 9QB
Royal Horticultural Society Garden, Wisley, Surrey GU23 6QB
Royal Botanic Gardens, Kew, Richmond, Surrey, TW9 3AE
Keele University, Staffordshire ST5 5BG

USA
Brooklyn Botanic Garden, Brooklyn, New York
New York Botanical Garden, Bronx, New York
US National Arboretum, Washington, DC.
Washington Park Arboretum, Seattle, Washington
San Francisco, California
Philadelphia, Pennsylvania

IN THE KITCHEN

I read recipes like I read science fiction. I get to the end and say to myself 'Well that's not going to happen'.

(Rita Rudner)

USING CHERRIES IN COOKING

There are two basic types of cherry: sweet and sour, sweet cherries having a higher sugar content. Don't be put off by the name; sour cherries aren't actually sour, they have a deeper more complex flavour and are better in some recipes. When looking for cherries to buy, be aware that sour cherries are mostly used in processed products, whereas the sweet versions are sold to be eaten fresh. If your recipe demands sour varieties you will probably need to grow them yourself or cultivate a friendly greengrocer to source them, that or fall back on bottled or frozen varieties. Luckily, many baking recipes can be adapted, and sweet cherries work perfectly well.

We learnt from Howard McGee, the guru on food science, that you can retain a firmer texture in certain fruits and vegetables, including cherries, by pre-cooking them at a low temperature. If you cook the fruit at 55-60 C / 130-140 F for 20-30 minutes it seems to 'set' the fruit and give a firmness which will last through further cooking. So, if you want your cherries to hold their shape in a casserole or compote, add in a pre-cooking step, and your final dish will then include 'whole' cherries. According to McGee, who understands these things, this is because cherries have an enzyme in their walls which becomes activated at around 50 C / 120 F (and turned off at higher temperatures) and alters the cell wall pectins, cross-linking them to calcium ions and making them resistant to removal or breakdown at high temperatures. Don't try to get your head round it, just remember, if you want a cherry purée or glaze go straight to boiling; if you would like some whole fruit in there cook a portion first at a lower heat. Remember though, this is kitchen science and temperatures should be correct, so use a thermometer.

Another interesting fact about cherries is that the rich source of phenolic antioxidants has a further benefit in that they make a natural flavour stabilizer. Dried cherries are rich in moisture retaining fibre and sorbitol, and so can be used in hamburgers and meatballs to replace fat and still keep a moist texture (no-one loves a dry meatball).

STONING FRUIT

Fortunately you can eat mulberries fresh, just as they come from the tree (although a very gentle rinse wouldn't hurt) but cherries, unless you are eating fresh or making toffeed cherries, will need to be stoned (pitted). The best way to do this is, unsurprisingly, with a cherry stoner (or an olive stoner, same thing really). Just take this device which looks a little like an instrument of medieval torture, sit the cherry on the cup, depress the plunger and the stone pops out leaving (provided your cherries are not overripe, in which case there is danger of mush) a largely whole but tooth-friendly fruit. If you don't have a cherry stoner you can use a knife; cut a slit in the side and flick the stone out. However, we wouldn't recommend this method if you have a choice – internet shopping means that your very own cherry stoner is only a click away and it takes up very little drawer space – because cherry flesh can adhere to the stone with the tenacity of a bulldog. In extremis, you can use a paperclip – yes you did read that right. Take a decent sized paperclip and open it out. Remove the stem of the cherry, insert one rounded end of the clip into the cherry where the stem came out, work it round the stone and then tug the stone out.

Whichever method you use, always stone (pit) your cherries over a bowl as you often get a lot of juice and it would be a pity to waste it.

Washing Fruit

Washing berries can be a bit of a minefield and this is especially so with mulberries which are extremely delicate. If they have come from higher branches on your own bush and you are confident they haven't been sprayed either by gardeners or passing dogs and foxes, then we would miss out the washing step altogether. There is always the danger of a little insect bonus, but these are harmless and don't stick in your teeth. If, however, your mulberries are a gift or a result of successful foraging, it might be just as well to give them a rinse; however proceed with caution. We find the best way is to fill a mixing bowl larger than your colander with cold water. Put the mulberries into the colander, don't pile then up too much as you don't want them to be crushed, then put the colander into the bowl and turn gently to swish the water and loosen any foreign bodies. Remove the colander and leave to drain.

Cherries are far more robust; however, it is best to wash them just before eating. Avoid washing before storage as water can accumulate in the hollow round the base of the stem (remember cherries store best on the stem) and encourage rot.

Storage

Sweet cherries won't ripen (just rot) after they have been picked and so their shelf life is limited. They keep best on the stem, but even then will only really last a couple of days. If any have come off their stems in the bag on the way home, eat those first, a cook's perk. Sour cherries, if you are lucky enough to get them, will last a little longer, up to a week kept in a paper bag in the refrigerator.

Luckily, however, both sorts freeze very well either stoned or with the stone in. Bear in mind if you are freezing them whole that the fruit will be softer once defrosted and removing the stone can be a messy business. We tend to freeze whole only those we are going to cook with the stone in.

When freezing whole cherries, wash and dry well and remove the stem. Line a baking tray (sheet) with baking paper and spread them out so they are not touching each other. Place in the freezer until frozen then bag up to store. For stoned fruit, wash and dry well, then remove the stones. Pack into rigid containers. Make up a light sugar syrup by heating two parts water to one part caster (superfine) sugar, stirring until the sugar is dissolved. Cool and pour over the stoned cherries and freeze.

Fresh mulberries are delicate and require careful handling; even in the fridge they will only last a day or two at best. When picked, you inevitably get a little bit of stem which comes with the berry. These are soft and don't really taste of anything so you can leave them in. If, however, you want to remove the stem for aesthetic reasons do not try to wrest it out with your fingers. The fruit will come off worst in this contest and you will end up with a squished berry. If you are making jam or jelly this isn't a problem, but if you are hoping for whole fruit then use either a pair of nail scissors or clippers and simply clip the stem off close to the fruit before using. If you are going to freeze the mulberries, do so stem on, as once frozen the stems easily snap off.

You can freeze mulberries but again they require careful handling. Line a baking tray (baking sheet) with baking paper and spread out the clean mulberries. If you have grown these yourself and are confident they have not been sprayed then forego washing; if you are less certain about the source, place in a colander and immerse in clean cold water, gently turn them, then lift out the colander and allow to drain. Give a final gentle pat dry before spreading out on the tray in a single layer not touching each other. Place the tray in the fast freeze section of your freezer for 2-3 hours to freeze, then pack the free flow fruit into plastic bags or rigid containers. They will keep in the freezer for up to six months. Use frozen berries in cakes and muffins or toss a handful into your morning smoothie. Defrosted they do lose their shape but are fine in pies, crumbles and cobblers. Frozen berries are just as good as fresh for making jams and jellies.

PROCESSED PRODUCTS

The universally appealing flavour of cherries has resulted in a myriad of processed cherry products being widely available: dried, bottled, canned, frozen, all have their uses in the kitchen and ensure that you can cook up cherry treats out of season. There are also lots of cherry flavoured confectionery, cookies and other lines, but surprisingly these do not always contain cherries. In processed foods, cherry flavour can come from almondy benzaldehyde and essence of cloves. It seems that proximity to almonds increases the cherryness of cherries, a fact often demonstrated in desserts and baking, which pair the two to mutual benefit.

Maraschino cherries were first produced in Dalmatia where the local Marasca cherry was preserved in cherry liqueur (made from the same fruit) for eating during the winter months. As with all products it is worth seeking out good quality versions of maraschino cherries. Industrially produced ones use lesser varieties of light skinned cherries, often bleached, that are stored in brine and then made up by pasteurising them, dying them red and packing them in a sugar syrup flavoured with almond essence. These can be cloyingly sweet and sickly.

We favour the Luxardo brand from Italy which is richly luscious. The liqueur is made from traditional Marasca cherries based on a recipe from 1821 and the cherries are bottled in the liqueur without any artificial colours or preservatives. The jars are around 50/50 cherries and syrup both of which are delicious. We used these in our chestnut cherry meringues (the recipe is in our book, *Nuts: Growing and Cooking*) and also in the Cherry Apple Strudel (see page 121). They are also amazing in cocktails, and a dash of the syrup in a glass of Coca Cola will result in a drink streets away from commercial cherry coke. They are stocked in good Italian delis or you can buy them over the internet. Technically, jars have a shelf life of three years but we have never been able to keep one long enough to confirm this.

Glacé cherries are a form of crystallized fruit, produced by taking whole cherries and soaking them in increasingly concentrated baths of heated sugar syrup over a period of several weeks. The syrup is absorbed by the fruit, driving out the moisture and preserving them. Doing this yourself would technically be possible but it is time consuming and messy, so we would recommend buying a good brand. The best glacé cherries are produced in Provence. These are the ones we used in our Cherry Cake (see page 148), Cherry Fudge (page 142) and in Cherry Ripe Bites (page 141).

Canned cherries are readily available. The favour is good but some brands can be very soft. They are best in a pie or for a sauce or purée.

Concentrated syrups of both cherries and mulberries are readily available and are invaluable in some recipes and when making cherry curd. Thick and sweet mulberry syrup is delicious drizzled over ice cream. Cherry concentrate is also a health product with a drink based on it helpful for arthritis and gout.

The one form you can easily find mulberries in is dried. They are readily available in health food shops, Mediterranean and Middle Eastern specialty shops, and some larger supermarkets. Dried mulberries are usually white mulberries. They have a delicate flavour and lend themselves well to Middle Eastern dishes. The one downside is their appearance. The dried mulberry's best friend would not describe it as a pretty fruit and it resembles most closely a small larval grub. Let us just say we would not recommend you garnishing a salad with them and leave it at that.

CHERRY DRINKS

There are two main types of cherry-based alcoholic products with differing flavours and uses.

Despite the name, cherry brandy is not in fact a distilled alcohol made from cherries, but rather a cherry-flavoured liqueur. The base spirit, usually vodka, is infused with cherries, cherry stones, or in cheaper brands flavoured with commercial extract and added sugar. A brand flavoured with cherry stones is a better choice – Bols is a good example – as they often have a slightly nutty flavour. It is higher-proof than many liqueurs, often approaching 80%. The well-known Dutch product Cherry Heering is aged in wooden barrels.

Cherry brandy has a slightly reddish colour and is sweet and slightly syrupy, with a hint of almonds. It is invaluable in cooking and is used in many cocktails including the Singapore Sling. Nigella Lawson uses cherry brandy in her sublime cranberry sauce recipe.

Kirsch or kirsch-wasser is a clear fruit brandy traditionally made from a double distillation of morello cherries, with no added sugar or flavourings. It is drier and subtler (what Jane would call more grown-up). The cherries are fermented on their stones and the best kirsch tastes both of cherries and a slightly bitter almond taste from the stones. It takes around 10 kilos / 22 pounds of cherries to make one 75 ml bottle of kirsch. It is believed to have originated in the Black Forest region of Germany and is traditionally used in Black Forest Gâteau.

In France it is known as eau de vie (eaux de vie come in a myriad of fruit flavours of which cerise is only one, check the picture on the bottle). Under EU law eaux de vie must have a minimum 37.5% ABV (75% proof), although kirsch is typically 80-100% proof. It is powerful stuff, so use sparingly.

BREAKFAST AND BRUNCH

Persian Toast with Mulberry Chutney

In a carpark beside the supermarket in Penclawdd, Wales, there is an unassuming kebab van run by a culinary genius. If you are ever passing through Penclawdd (yes we know, but it could happen, we were) you must stop at Baraka. The food is all freshly prepared and served with homemade sauces, and the kebabs are amazing, but the breakfast is a revelation. Persian toast, a spicy version of eggy bread, is absolutely delicious. This is our version, and we have taken it even further with a mulberry chutney and yoghurt. Next time you fancy a bit of eastern promise at breakfast try this.

The mulberry chutney makes a little more than you need, but the rest will not go to waste: you can stir it into yoghurt or serve it on hot buttered toast like an exotic, if a bit runny, jam. Use sourdough or a good country bread – supermarket white sliced bread will just disintegrate. If you can get powdered dried lime it gives an authentic, smoky-sour flavour. You should be able to get it online or from a Middle Eastern deli, but if not just miss it out.

Serves 2

75 g / 2 ½ oz dried mulberries
75 g / 2 ½ oz sultanas (golden raisins)

150 g / 5 oz / ⅔ cup golden caster sugar
500 ml / 16 fl oz / 2 cups water
juice of a lime
2 thick slices of good white bread
2 eggs, beaten
1 teaspoon turmeric
½ teaspoon ground cumin
½ teaspoon dried lime (optional)
1 red chilli, chopped
2 tablespoons of fresh coriander, finely chopped
knob of butter
thick Greek yoghurt to serve

Wash a 250 ml / 8 fl oz / 1 cup jar and place in a low oven to dry. Cover the mulberries and sultanas with boiling water and leave for about half an hour to plump up. Drain. Put into a heavy-bottomed saucepan with the sugar and 500 ml / 16 fl oz / 2 cups of water. Bring to the boil, reduce the heat and simmer for 40-45 minutes, stirring occasionally until thickened slightly and the syrup coats the back of a spoon. Stir in the lime juice. Pour into the jar and seal whilst hot. Stored in a cool place out of direct sunlight this can keep for up to a year.

In a wide, shallow dish beat the eggs and stir in the spices, chilli and coriander. Lay the bread in the egg mix, leave for a few minutes then turn over. Leave another few minutes to absorb the spicy eggy mix.

Heat a large heavy-bottomed frying pan (skillet) and add the knob of butter. When the butter is sizzling add the eggy bread and fry (sauté) for a few minutes until golden and crispy round the edges. Flip to cook the other side. Once cooked serve immediately with a large spoonful of mulberry preserve and some thick yoghurt.

CHERRY BLINTZES

These are a lovely dessert or an unusual and delicious addition to brunch.

Serves 4

100 g / 3 oz / ¾ cup plain (all purpose) flour
1 egg
1 tablespoon caster (superfine) sugar
½ teaspoon salt
300 ml / 10 fl oz / 1 ¼ cups milk
1 tablespoon butter, melted, plus more to cook pancakes
675 g / 1 lb 6 oz / 3 cups fresh cherries, pitted
125 ml / 4 fl oz / ½ cup water
125 g / 4 oz / ½ cup caster (superfine) sugar
225 g / 8 oz / 1 cup cream cheese
125 g / 4 oz / ½ cup mascarpone
2 tablespoon caster (superfine) sugar
1 teaspoon cinnamon
1 teaspoon cornflour (cornstarch)

Sift the flour into a bowl, make a well in the centre and add the egg. Beat to combine, then gradually add the milk and melted butter until you have a pourable batter the consistency of cream.

Heat a teaspoon of butter in a small frying pan (skillet) or crêpe pan. Once the butter is sizzling ladle in just enough batter to coat the bottom of the pan. Cook until set and just starting to colour. Flip (if you are brave) or turn and cook the second side for a minute. Remove from the pan. Repeat until you have used up the batter, stacking the pancakes with a piece of baking paper between each one to avoid sticking. You can do this in advance and store in the fridge overnight or freeze until you are ready to use.

Put the cherries, sugar and water in a heavy-bottomed saucepan. Bring to the boil and simmer gently for 5 minutes until the cherries are soft but still have some shape. Take a little of the juice out of the pan and mix with the cornflour (cornstarch) to form a paste. Stir back into the cherries and stir over the heat for a couple of minutes to thicken the cherry sauce. Set aside and keep warm until the blintzes are ready.

Mix the cheese, mascarpone, sugar and cinnamon. Take one pancake, place a generous heaped tablespoon of filling in the middle. Fold both sides to the centre and then fold up the ends to give a neat parcel. Make up the rest of the pancake parcels in the same manner.

Heat a tablespoon of butter in a pan and fry the parcels until golden and the pancakes just starting to crisp on the edges.

Serve with the cherry sauce poured over.

MAIN COURSES

VENISON WITH RED WINE AND CHERRY SAUCE

Here the rich sweet cherry sauce acts as the perfect accent to the gamey venison. You can leave the steaks whole and just pour over the sauce, but we prefer to cut the meat across the grain to form a pile of juicy fragments of tender meat.

In summer you should use fresh sour or morello cherries, but at other times of the year frozen cherries or dried sour cherries soaked for an hour in boiling water then drained work perfectly well.

Serve with potato gratin and green beans.

Serves 4

600 ml / 1 pint / 2 ½ cups beef stock
300 ml / 10 fl oz red wine
dash of olive oil
2 shallots
1 clove garlic
200 g / 7 oz / about 20 sour or morello cherries
1 tablespoon cranberry sauce or cherry ginger chutney (see page 110)
25 g / 1 oz / 2 tablespoons butter
1 tablespoon fresh chopped tarragon
4 small venison steaks (approx. 150 g each)

Put the stock and wine in a saucepan and boil rapidly to reduce by half.

Prepare the ingredients for the sauce. Chop the shallots and garlic finely. Stone the cherries and cut in half.

Heat a heavy-bottomed frying pan (skillet) to high heat. Season and then sear the steaks for 2-3 minutes each side until cooked medium rare (or to your preference). Remove, wrap in foil and keep warm whilst you make the sauce.

Turn down the heat to low and add a dash of oil to the pan and fry (sauté) the shallots and garlic until tender but not coloured. Add the cherries to the pan. Pour in the wine reduction, increase the heat and simmer till thickened slightly. Whisk in the cranberry sauce and butter to form a smooth sauce.

Unwrap the steaks and slice if you like or place the whole steaks on plates. Pour over the sauce and serve immediately.

Stuffed Pork Fillet

This makes a useful quick Sunday lunch for unexpected guests with the tasty stuffing stretching a single pork fillet out to feed six.

Serves 4-6

1 pork fillet (tenderloin)
250 g / 8 oz sausage meat
20 g / ½ oz / 1 ½ tablespoons dried sour cherries
20 g / ½ oz / ¼ cup fresh breadcrumbs
2 tablespoons parsley
1 tablespoon thyme leaves
80 g / 3 oz / approx. 6 slices prosciutto crudo
knob of butter
1 shallot
3 tablespoons cherry brandy
250 ml / 8 fl oz / 1 cup chicken stock
10 cherries (about half a cup), stoned and halved

Preheat the oven to 220 C / 425 F / Gas 7.

Chop the cherries and parsley. Mix with the sausage meat, thyme and breadcrumbs and season well.

Remove any silver skin from the pork fillet (tenderloin) and cut a slit along the long edge opening the meat out like a book. Beat to flatten slightly and even up. Lay out the prosciutto on an oven tray to form an even rectangle. Lay the pork on top of the prosciutto and place the stuffing mix in a line down the centre. Roll up into a cylinder with the prosciutto slices around the outside. Put onto a baking tray and roast for 10 minutes.

Turn the oven down to 190 C / 375 F / Gas 5 and roast for a further 20-25 minutes or until cooked through. Rest for 5-10 minutes while you make the sauce.

Soften a shallot in a knob of butter. Add cherry brandy and cook until reduced down to nearly nothing. Add chicken stock and any of the pan juices and reduce by half. Add the cherries and warm through. Serve the pork sliced into medallions and sprinkle with sauce.

CHERRIES & MULBERRIES

Mulberry and Pine nut Kibbeh

This Persian-inspired recipe makes a great lunch or supper dish served with couscous and a green salad. The mulberry pine nut butter centre keeps the kibbeh moist. The best results, we think, are achieved if you deep fry the kibbeh which is traditional, but if you prefer not to deep fry we have given an oven baked option.

Serves 4

½ onion
300 g / 10 oz lamb mince
150 g / 4 oz bulgur wheat
1 clove of garlic, crushed
½ teaspoon cinnamon
½ teaspoon allspice
1 teaspoon Aleppo chilli flakes
75 g / 2 ½ oz / ⅔ stick butter
30 g / 1 oz pine nuts
30 g / 1 oz dried mulberries, chopped
½ teaspoon of cinnamon
125 ml / 4 fl oz / ½ cup natural yoghurt
1 tablespoon of tahini
squeeze of lemon juice

Soak the bulgur wheat in cold water for 15 minutes, then drain and squeeze out any remaining water.

Whizz the raw onion in a processor until it is a purée. Add the lamb, garlic and spices and whizz again. You want the mince to be very finely ground, more a paste than a mince texture. Add the bulgur and whizz to combine. Put the meat paste into the fridge for half an hour to chill down.

Fry (sauté) the pine nuts for a couple of minutes until golden. Cool. Soften the butter in a bowl and mix in the mulberries, pine nuts and cinnamon.

Divide the meat mixture into 16 equally sized balls. Using your thumb make an indentation in each ball, place a knob of the spiced butter in the indentation and fold the meat round to make a ball. To be truly authentic you should shape the balls into ovals with slightly pointy ends, but they will still taste delicious shaped like conventional meatballs. Put aside in the fridge until you are ready to cook them.

Make the sauce by combining the yoghurt, tahini and lemon juice. Season to taste. If it is too thick, add a little water to make a drizzling consistency.

If you are oven baking then preheat the oven to 190 C / 375 F / Gas 5. If frying, heat a pan of oil until a cube of bread browns. Bake the kibbeh for 20 minutes or fry for 3-4 minutes until browned and crunchy on the outside and cooked through.

Serve drizzled with sauce and accompanied by a crisp green salad.

Venison Burgers with Fresh Cherry Relish

You can tweak the burger "fixings" to suit your own taste: use blue cheese instead of cheddar, add gherkins, leave out the avocado. However, we are adamant that you use proper buns (rolls), this modern preference for brioche rolls is just not right, they are, in our opinion, far too sweet. You can also use beef (or indeed pork) for the patties although the venison complements the fresh cherry relish beautifully, making a lovely summer burger perfect for an afternoon barbecue. The bacon is essential for venison burgers as venison is a very lean meat which can be a little springy in texture if used alone, with beef or pork it is optional but tasty.

Serves 6

For the burger patties
30 g / 1 oz streaky bacon
½ red onion, finely chopped
350 g / 12 oz venison mince (ground venison)
30 g / 1 oz / ¼ cup fresh breadcrumbs

1 egg, beaten
salt and pepper

For the relish
1 tablespoon olive or rapeseed oil
1 banana shallot, finely chopped
1 clove garlic, crushed
1 cup fresh cherries, pitted and chopped
1 tablespoon finely grated fresh ginger
2 tablespoons fresh parsley, finely chopped
juice half a lime
1 teaspoon sherry vinegar
salt and pepper to taste

1 tablespoon mayonnaise
mixed salad leaves
2 plum tomatoes, sliced
½ cup mixed spouts (chickpea, lentil, radish etc)
150 g / 5 oz cheddar cheese
2 avocados, sliced
6 baps or burger buns

Chop the bacon very finely, you are aiming for the same textures as the mince (ground meat). Mix together the bacon, onion, mince (ground meat), breadcrumbs and egg. Season well with salt and pepper. Form into 6 substantial patties, make them slightly wider than the buns as they will shrink a little on cooking. Put in the fridge for half an hour to firm up.

Whilst the patties are resting, make the relish. Mix all the relish ingredients together and leave to rest to allow the flavours to develop.

When you are ready to eat, cook the patties on a barbecue grill or ridged pan for 5 minutes each side or until cooked to your preference.

Toast the buns on the same grill. Spread the bottom half of the bun with the mayonnaise. Fill with salad leaves, tomatoes and sprouts. Top with a meat pattie, a slice of cheese, the avocado and a generous spoonful of relish. Top with the other half of the bun and serve with chips and salad.

Barbecued Beans

The spirit of serendipity in the shape of Ian scouring the fridge for breakfast fixings led us to this recipe. He used a tin of Heinz baked beans and a quarter of a cup of sauce, and in extremis you can of course do this too, but if you go to the trouble of making your own beans it will be all the more delicious. We have used tinned beans but if you have the time (and foresight) soak a cup of haricot or pinto beans overnight, drain and boil in fresh water (no salt, this would toughen the beans) for 40 minutes to an hour or until tender but not mushy, and then follow the recipe.

Serves 2-3

1 tablespoon olive oil
1 red onion
2 cloves garlic
1 tablespoon red wine vinegar
1 tablespoon soft brown sugar
400 g / 14 oz can pinto beans, drained and rinsed
400 g / 14 oz can of chopped tomatoes
½ cup tangy barbecue sauce (see page 116)

Halve the red onion and cut into thin half-moons. Heat the oil in a heavy-bottomed frying pan (skillet) and fry (sauté) until soft and translucent, add the garlic and fry for a minute or two more or until fragrant. Add the vinegar and sugar and cook until the onions are nicely caramelized. Stir in the beans, chopped tomatoes and barbecue sauce and cook together for 15 minutes until slightly thickened. Taste and season.

Serve them on wholemeal toast for breakfast or alongside sausages or steak to channel your inner cowboy.

Chicken Liver and Cherry Parfait with Crispy Glaze

This makes a really impressive starter or shared lunch. The pâté is silky smooth and slightly sweet, offset by the cherry glaze just sharpened by the balsamic, but what makes it really special is the crispy caramel glaze. It is very slightly Heston Blumenthal and you can miss it off and it will still be delicious, but if you want to do impressive pyrotechnics (and we all do sometimes) then do try it, it doesn't take long. A word of warning though, you will need a blowtorch and use it at the last minute. If you do it ahead of time it will dissolve into a pool of caramel, which is not what you want. You must be quick in melting the sugar, hence the blowtorch, if you try to do it under a grill you will just melt the jelly glaze.

You can make this in one dish to put on a lunch table, or in small ramekins to make individual entrée (appetiser) size portions.

Gelatine leaves vary in size depending on the brand, so measure the cherry balsamic liquid and adjust the quantity of gelatine according to packet instructions if required.

Serves 6-8

250 g / 8 oz / 2 sticks butter
400 g / 14 oz chicken livers
1 teaspoon sea salt
½ teaspoon ground allspice
leaves from 3 sprigs of thyme
1 tablespoon Bourbon
2 tablespoons maple syrup
2 tablespoons cherry brandy
1 sheet leaf gelatine
125 g / 4 oz fresh or frozen cherries, pitted
30 g / 1 oz caster (superfine) sugar
75 ml / 2 ½ fl oz / ¼ cup water
1 teaspoon balsamic vinegar
2-3 tablespoons granulated sugar

Trim the chicken livers, removing any gristly bits. Melt 50 g / 1 ¾ oz of butter in a large heavy-bottomed frying pan (skillet) and fry (sauté) the livers, salt, allspice and thyme briefly over a high heat for 3 minutes until well browned but still a little pink inside. Remove from the heat and add the Bourbon and maple syrup and stir through the livers.

Put into a food processor, add the cherry brandy and one third of the butter. Whiz to combine. Add another third of the butter and whizz again. Add the last measure of butter and give a final whizz. The mixture should be smooth with no lumps. Pass through a metal sieve to ensure it is completely silky. Normally we don't favour extra sieving steps, keeping our terrine, pâtés and soups rustic, but for the parfait you really want the silky texture so it is worth the extra effort.

Put into a dish (we use a shallow 12 cm / 5 inch round dish) cover with cling film (saran wrap) and put in the fridge to set.

Put the gelatine leaf in water to soften. Put the cherries, sugar and water in a saucepan, bring to the boil and simmer for 3 minutes. Remove from the heat and cool just slightly, you want it warm enough to dissolve the gelatine. Add gelatine and stir to dissolve. Pour over the pâté and return to the fridge to set.

Just before you want to serve, sprinkle the surface with sugar, fire up your blowtorch and caramelize the sugar. Work quickly as you don't want to melt the jelly.

Serve with crackers or melba toast.

SALADS AND SIDES

Sorrel Pilaf with Caramelized Fennel and Dried Mulberries

This Persian-inspired side dish is delicious with fish, perhaps a tuna or swordfish steak sprinkled with a little oil and za'atar and griddled or barbecued. The sorrel gives a lovely lemony freshness, but if you can't get it (farmers markets or fish shops often have it and it is easy to grow) then use spinach.

Serves 4 as side dish

1 medium fennel bulb
1 onion
3 tablespoons oil
300 g / 10 oz bulgur wheat
600 ml / 1 pint / 2 ½ cups chicken or fish stock
40 g / 1 ½ oz / ¼ cup dried mulberries
60 g / 2 oz fresh sorrel leaves

Finely slice the fennel, reserving any feathery fronds. Finely slice the onion. Sauté the fennel and onion in one tablespoon of oil over a low heat for 15-20 minutes until golden and caramelized.

In a separate pan, heat another tablespoon of oil, add the bulgur and stir until well coated. Add the stock, bring to the boil and simmer until the liquid is absorbed. Taste it, the grains should be tender but not mushy. Stir in the caramelized fennel.

Roll and shred the sorrel leaves. Stir the mulberries and sorrel into the pilaf and allow the heat just to wilt the leaves. Taste and adjust seasoning if required.

GREEN SALAD WITH CHERRIES AND WALNUTS

A simple green salad which partners really well with smoked meats or game. If you want a stronger fruity taste then use the mulberry dressing recipe which follows, substituting cherry concentrate for mulberry.

Serves 4

12 cherries (approximately ½ cup), pitted and halved
mixed salad leaves
12 walnuts or pecans, lightly toasted

3 tablespoons olive or rapeseed oil
1 tablespoon cider vinegar
1 teaspoon nigella seeds

Wash and thoroughly dry the salad leaves. Add the remaining salad ingredients. Mix the dressing ingredients together and whisk to emulsify. Toss the salad with dressing and serve.

Mulberry Dressing

Mulberry concentrate gives a sweet-sour fruity flavour similar to pomegranate molasses. This dressing is ideal to lift a simple green salad on a Middle Eastern buffet table. We have given a small amount to dress a large bowl of green leaves, but by all means scale up and make a large jar. It will keep well in the fridge but let it come up to room temperature before you use it and give a good shake to emulsify.

3 tablespoons rapeseed or olive oil
1 tablespoon sherry vinegar
1 tablespoon mulberry concentrate
½ teaspoon Dijon mustard
salt and pepper to taste

Cherries & Mulberries

Put all the ingredients in a screw-top jar and shake well to emulsify. Pour or drizzle over your salad.

Smoked Duck and Cherry Salad

In Wales we visited Jo and Jonathan Carthew at the Black Mountains smokery near Crickhowell. They produce a fabulous range of smoked meats and cheeses. One of our favourites was the smoked duck, which inspired this recipe. If you can get hold of smoked sea salt do use this on the beetroot (beets) when you roast them, it adds a lovely smokey dimension, but if you don't have any to hand then good sea salt will do.

Serves 4 for light lunch

1 smoked duck breast
4 small beetroot (beets)
1 tablespoon oil
2 tablespoons balsamic vinegar
2 good sprinkles of sea salt (smoked if possible)
½ teaspoon smoked paprika
1 cup cherries, stoned
¼ cup pecans
bag of rocket

Preheat the oven to 200 C / 400 F / Gas 6. Peel the beetroot (beets) and cut into quarters or eighths according to size. Put into an oven dish and drizzle with oil and balsamic. Cover with foil and bake for one hour or until tender.

Toast the pecans in a dry pan until they start to smell nutty. Remove from the pan and toss with smoked paprika and salt.

Slice the duck breast finely. Place the rocket onto a decorative platter. Top with the beetroot (beets), sliced duck and cherries. Season to taste. Drizzle with more balsamic and oil to taste.

STORE CUPBOARD PRESERVES

CHERRY GINGER CHUTNEY

This is a warm sweet rich chutney which is just made for ham. Make a few jars at Christmas as gifts, as it will go perfectly with Christmas cold cuts. We like to use a few dried cherries in with the fresh as it adds a little body and helps thicken the chutney. Like most chutneys it matures in the jar and will taste better if you can leave it a month before using it.

You can fish the star anise and whole chillies out before you jar this or leave in to enrich the flavour – just remember, these are not intended to be eaten.

If you are making this outside of cherry season then frozen work just fine.

Makes 600 g / 1 ¼ lbs

500 g / 1 lb / 2 ½ cups fresh or frozen cherries, pitted
150 g / 5 oz / 1 ½ cups dried cherries
2 onions
150 ml / 5 fl oz / ⅔ cup sherry vinegar
150 ml / 5 fl oz / ⅔ cup red wine or port
1-2 whole dried chillies
250 g / 8 oz / 1 cup soft brown sugar
1 tablespoon mustard seeds
2 star anise
1 tablespoon freshly grated ginger

Wash the jars thoroughly in warm soapy water, rinse well and place in a very low oven to dry thoroughly.

Peel and finely chop the onions. Put everything into a large non-reactive saucepan on a low heat. Heat gently, stirring until the sugar has completely dissolved. Increase the heat and bring up to a gentle simmer. Cover and cook for 10 minutes until the onion has softened.

Remove the lid and cook for 45-50 minutes until thick. You can remove the whole chillies and star anise at this point or leave them in the jars.

Rest for 5 minutes, then fill the jars and seal. Put in a cool dark place and ideally keep for a month before using.

Mulberry Jelly

This makes a beautiful jewel-coloured jelly. You can eat it on toast, like jam, or serve with game meats. If you think you are only going to use it for savoury dishes then you can pop a small split chilli or whole star anise in each jar to give it a little bit of an extra kick. The key to a clear jelly is patience, you need to wait for it to drip through the jelly bag, if you try to rush it with a surreptitious squeeze it will be cloudy. Don't bother taking all those pesky stalks out of the mulberries, they will be strained out when you put the jelly through the muslin.

Makes 8 x 250 g / ½ lb jars

1.5 kg / 3 lb mulberries
½ cup freshly squeezed lemon juice
1.5 kg / 3 lb / 7 cups granulated sugar
175 g / 6 oz pectin
knob of butter

Wash your jars thoroughly in warm soapy water, rinse well and place in a very low oven to dry thoroughly.

Whizz the mulberries in a food processor. Put in a large saucepan, bring to the boil and simmer for 15 minutes. Strain through muslin or a jelly bag over a large saucepan. Leave this to drip through at its own pace, if you hurry it through you will end up with cloudy jelly.

Add the sugar and lemon juice and stir to dissolve the sugar. Bring back to the boil and boil hard for 10 minutes. Add the knob of butter and stir – this will remove the foam on the top of the jelly. Now add your pectin, bring back to the boil and boil for 1 minute. Remove from the heat and ladle into the clean sterilized jars.

PICKLED CHERRIES

These are easy to make and will last a year or more. They are ideal with pâtés, cold meats and cheeses. and make perfect picnic fare. The key is to use firm raw fruit and ensure the pickling liquid is quite cool before pouring over, to ensure the fruit does not cook and become soft.

Makes 2 x 400 ml / 14 oz jars

350 g / 12 oz / 1 ½ cups golden caster (superfine) sugar
400 ml / 14 fl oz white wine vinegar
1 tablespoon black peppercorns
4 whole cloves
2 bay leaves
500 g / 1 lb / 2 cups whole cherries

Carefully wash the jars and place in the oven at the lowest possible heat to dry. Heat the sugar and vinegar gently in a non-reactive saucepan, stirring until the sugar dissolves. Add the spices and simmer for 10 minutes. Cool completely.

Wash and dry the cherries and trim the stalks to just above the fruit. Pack into the hot sterile jars and pour over the cooled pickling solution. Seal the jars and keep in a cool dark place for at least a month before eating.

BRANDIED CHERRIES

With a jar of these in the cupboard you have an instant dessert – just add vanilla ice cream. Remember the juice and sauce is vital here, so whilst you don't have to use finest cognac pick a brandy you are happy to drink.

1 kg / 2 lb / 4 cups whole cherries
1 cinnamon stick
300 g / 10 oz / 1 ⅓ cups golden caster (superfine) sugar

750 ml / 1 ½ pints / 3 cups of brandy

Wash your jars carefully and place in a low oven to dry. Wash and dry the fruit and trim the stems. Sterilize a sharp darning needle and prick each cherry several times. Place the fruit into the hot jars.

Take 1 cup of brandy and place in a saucepan with the sugar. Heat gently, stirring until the sugar dissolves. Try not to let it boil. Once the sugar has dissolved, remove from the heat, add the rest of the brandy and pour over the cherries, ensuring they are all submerged. Seal the jars and keep in a cool dark place for at least a month before using.

MULBERRY LIQUEUR

A mulberry flavoured liqueur akin to crème de cassis which is totally delicious and not to be confused with myr, which is made with bilberries, or mûre with blackberries. If you can get hold of a bottle of Caruso e Minini Perricone, a red wine made in Sicily which really does taste of mulberries, this would be perfect.

500 g / 1 lb mulberries
750 ml / 1 ½ pints / 3 cups red wine
750 g / 1 ½ lb / 3 ⅓ cups caster (superfine) sugar
375 ml / ¾ pint / 1 ⅔ cups brandy, gin or vodka

Soak the mulberries in red wine for 48 hours. Whizz in a food processor. Line a bowl with muslin or a clean J cloth. Tip the mulberry mix into the bowl. Pick up the muslin and pull the edges together and twist to squeeze out all the liquid into the bowl.

Measure the liquid and put into a preserving pan. Add 1 kg / 2 lb / 5 cups sugar for each litre of liquid. Stir over a low heat until the sugar is dissolved. Hold below boiling point for 15 minutes stirring constantly. Leave the mixture on a very low heat, stirring every now and again until reduced. After two hours the liquid will be reduced and syrupy. Cool.

Measure and add one cup of spirit to each 3 cups of syrup. Bottle. You can use it immediately or it will keep for at least a year.

Sugar Cubes for Champagne Cocktails

This is one for our friend Annette, a woman who likes the finer things in life and whose fridge so often contains a bottle of champagne. Not at all the reason we visit, of course. These pretty little cubes add sparkle and a girly pinkness to a champagne cocktail. In fact if you want to go the whole Disney princess thing, then use heart shape moulds for ultimate romantic prettiness.

You can make your own mulberry syrup by boiling up equal amounts of sugar and mulberries, straining and then reducing by one half to a syrup consistency. Or do like we do and buy a bottle readymade.

125 g / 4 oz / 1 cup icing (confectioners') sugar
1 tablespoon mulberry syrup

Sieve the sugar into a bowl to remove any lumps. Mix in the mulberry syrup gradually. You may need a little more or a little less, you are looking for the consistency of wet sand. Pack into silicon moulds either sugar lump sized square ones (look for cubette ice cube trays) or small heart-shaped ones. Remember small is the key here, you want a cube which will sit nicely in the bottom of a champagne flute. Leave overnight to dry out.

We have heard that you can accelerate the drying process by giving the tray a brief blast (thirty seconds) in the microwave first, but as neither of us has any truck with microwaves we haven't tested this. Just waiting till tomorrow works for us.

Mulberry Shrub

A shrub is a sweet-sour syrup used as a base for cocktails or mixed drinks. Foraged shrubs are just so on trend at the moment and a mulberry shrub is delicious.

The term comes from the Arabic word *sharbah* meaning drink and similar vinegar based drinks have been around since the Babylonians. Colonial sailors used to take shrub syrups with them on long voyages to combat scurvy. They were also tremendously popular during temperance periods in the nineteenth and twentieth centuries.

Traditionally you mix one to two tablespoons of shrub syrup into a long glass of soda water for a healthy and refreshing drink. If, however, you add a generous shot of gin you have mulberry gin fizz and trust us, on a summer afternoon this knocks a G&T for six. You can also mix shrub syrup with olive oil for a fruity salad dressing.

Makes approx 600 ml / 1 pint

200 g / 7 oz / 1 cup fresh or frozen mulberries
squeeze of lemon juice
100 g / 3 ½ oz / ½ cup granulated sugar
250 ml / 8 fl oz / 1 cup apple cider vinegar

Whizz the mulberries in a blender to make a purée. Put the fruit in a heavy-bottomed pan over a medium heat. Heat gently, stirring to dissolve the sugar. Remove from the heat. Add the vinegar and leave to infuse for a minimum of 24 hours and up to three days.

Strain, discard any fruit pulp (and those pesky stems). Bottle in a clean sterilized bottle and keep in the fridge for up to six months. In the unlikely event of the mixture beginning to bubble and ferment, discard it. In fact we find this to be a useful universal rule for fridge maintenance, if it bubbles and hisses throw it out.

Mix one to two tablespoons of shrub syrup with a glass of still or sparkling water for a refreshing drink.

Cherry Sangria

When you are bored with Pimms, then it is the moment for cherry sangria. This is prettily pink and perfect for picnics or summer barbecues. You can leave the cherries whole, just warn your guests about the stones, or pit them and sit back and relax.

750 ml / 20 fl oz / 1 bottle rose wine
250 ml / 8 fl oz / 1 cup sour cherry juice
250 ml / 8 fl oz / 1 cup orange juice (ideally freshly-squeezed)
60 ml / 2 fl oz / ¼ cup kirsch
1 cup fresh cherries, pitted
1 orange
soda water (club soda) to taste

Take the orange and slice thinly. Discard the two ends, the bits with all the peel on them, rather than just a thin ring. Mix all the other ingredients together and put in a pretty jug with ice cubes.

Pour into glasses and top up with soda to taste.

Tangy Barbecue Sauce

This sweet, tangy barbecue sauce is an essential addition to your summer cooking repertoire. You can use it to glaze chops, chicken, ribs, pretty much anything you care to barbecue. You could, if you are cooking for children, omit the bourbon but we feel it would be a pity; just give them some plain sausages. We have also given you a recipe for glazed burgers and one for beans using the sauce, you will find both in the main course section.

Makes 1 ½ cups of sauce

1 tablespoon olive oil
½ onion, finely chopped
1 tablespoon smoked paprika
250 ml / 8 fl oz / 1 cup cherry coke
250 ml / 8 fl oz / 1 cup tomato ketchup
60 ml / 2 fl oz / ¼ cup Worcester sauce
2 tablespoons dark brown sugar
60 ml / 2 fl oz / ¼ cup Bourbon

Wash your jar or bottle thoroughly in hot soapy water and place in the oven on a low heat to dry. Fry (sauté) the onion in the oil until soft and translucent. Add the smoked paprika, stir well to coat the onion. Add the remaining ingredients. Stir well, bring to the boil and simmer for 15 minutes to thicken. Season to taste. Use or bottle in a sterilized jar where it will keep for at least a year.

CHERRY COKE

We find commercial cherry coke a great ingredient – see our recipe for barbecue sauce (page 116), and Nigella has a fantastic recipe for whole ham cooked in cherry coke. However, when it comes to a refreshing glass of fizzy pop it really is just too artificial tasting. We find it much nicer to use a quarter of a cup of cherry syrup and top up with soda water (club soda) and a slice of lemon. Alternatively, make a bottle of our base syrup below, which includes ginger and brown sugar for that caramelly kick. Keep this in the fridge and again just top up the glass with soda to taste.

A glass of cherry cola poured over a scoop of vanilla ice cream makes an amazing cherry float.

Makes about 3 cups

600 ml / 1 pint / 2 ½ cups water
750 g / 1 ½ lbs cherries, pitted
200 g / 7 oz / 1 cup white sugar
250 g / 8 oz / 1 cup brown sugar
zest 1 orange
zest 1 lemon
1 cinnamon stick
a knob of fresh ginger peeled and sliced

Put all the ingredients in a heavy-bottomed pan. Heat gently, stirring to dissolve the sugar. Bring to the boil and simmer for 30 minutes until the cherries are completely soft. Mash up with a wooden spoon. Strain through muslin and discard the solids. Bottle and keep in the fridge.

CHERRY CURD

This is a beautiful, delicately flavoured summer curd, the perfect topping for our cherry scones (see page 156). As this contains eggs and butter it is best made in small quantities and must be kept in the fridge. If possible take it out of the fridge half an hour before use to allow it to come to room temperature, as the butter makes the texture a little grainy if served fridge-cold.

Sieving the eggs may seem like a bit of a faff but it ensures there are no lumps of albumen and gives you a smoother curd that is far less likely to scramble.

If you want this to be prettily pink you will need to add a few drops of pink food colouring at the end, otherwise it will be a little dull in colour although still delicious.

Concentrated cherry juice is available from health food shops or online.

Makes 350-400 ml / 10-14 fl oz

⅓ cup of concentrated cherry juice
1 tablespoon cherry brandy
225 g / 8 oz / 1 cup caster sugar
115 g / 4 oz / ½ stick butter
2 eggs
pinch of salt (if using unsalted butter)
a few drops of pink food colouring

To sterilize the jars first preheat the oven to 110 C / 225 F / Gas ¼. Wash the jars and lids thoroughly in hot soapy water and rinse well. You can run them through a cycle of the dishwasher if you prefer. Put the jars upside down in the oven. If you are using metal lids they can go in the oven too. Drying the jars in the oven removes the risk of wiping them with a less than spotless cloth and by the time the curd is ready they should be totally dry. Leave in the oven until the curd is cooked as this will keep them hot and less likely to crack when you pour the hot liquid into them.

Finely dice the butter. Beat the eggs and pass them through a metal sieve. Put everything except the food colouring in a heavy-bottomed pan. Heat very gently over a low heat, stirring continuously to dissolve the sugar and melt the butter. Keep stirring and cook for 10-15 minutes until the mixture thickens as much as you dare, it should coat the back of a spoon and allow you to draw a clear line through it. Do not leave this unattended or be tempted to turn up the heat. This will result in cherry flavoured scrambled eggs, definitely an acquired taste.

Pour into the jars and keep in the fridge.

MULBERRY CURD

Another way of making curd, this uses cream instead of butter and has the advantage of not going grainy in the fridge. We owe the idea from Thane Prince in her excellent book *Perfect Preserves*. We think the traditional version (above) is slightly nicer on scones, but this makes a beautiful tartlet filling. Just make (or buy) some little tartlet cases and fill with a few spoonfuls of mulberry curd and top with a nice fat mulberry. These make a delicious addition to afternoon tea or a little sweet canapé.

Makes 350-400 ml / 10-14 fl oz

⅓ cup concentrated mulberry juice or mulberry syrup
115 g / 4 oz / ½ caster (superfine) sugar
100 ml / 3 ½ fl oz / ⅓ cup double (heavy) cream
2 large eggs
1 tablespoon crème de mure or crème de cassis
a few drops of purple food colouring (optional)

To sterilize the jars first preheat the oven to 110 C / 225 F / Gas ¼. Wash the jars and lids thoroughly in hot soapy water and rinse well. You can run them through a cycle of the dishwasher if you prefer. Put the jars upside down in the oven. If you are using metal lids they can go in the oven too. Drying the jars in the oven removes the risk of wiping them with a less than spotless cloth and by the time the curd is ready they should be totally dry. Leave in the oven until the curd is cooked as this will keep them hot and less likely to crack when you pour the hot liquid into them.

Beat the eggs and pass them through a metal sieve. Put everything except the food colouring in a heavy-bottomed pan. Heat very gently over a low heat, stirring continuously to dissolve the sugar. Keep stirring and cook for 10-15 minutes, until the mixture thickens as much as you dare. It should coat the back of a spoon and allow you to draw a clear line through it. Do not leave it unattended or turn up the heat as it may scramble.

Fill the sterilized jars with curd and seal. This should be kept refrigerated.

PIES AND TARTS

Cherries and mulberries are simply made for pastry. They seem to suit all sorts, from filo through to hot water crust. Here are a selection of our favourite pies and tarts using our favourite fruit.

CHERRY APPLE STRUDEL

On holiday in Budapest we fell in love with cherry strudel (it's research not gluttony, darling). There it is made with proper strudel dough, a thin pastry made from flour, water, oil and salt, but we found that filo pastry makes a very acceptable alternative. In Budapest they often serve this with a poppyseed ice cream, which is delicious.

In season, you can make a complete cherry strudel using fresh cherries. This recipe was developed when we wanted a cherry dessert in April (lots of beautiful blossom but no cherries yet). It is so delicious you can make it at anytime. Serve with gently whipped cream.

Serves 3-4

6 sheets of filo pastry
35 g / 1 ¼ oz / 2 ½ tablespoons butter
450 g / 15 oz jar maraschino cherries in syrup
2 eating apples
3 tablespoons ground almonds
3 tablespoons fresh breadcrumbs
2 tablespoons demerara (raw) sugar, plus a little extra to sprinkle
1 tablespoon cornflour (cornstarch)

Drain the cherries, reserving the syrup. Melt the butter. Mix the breadcrumbs, ground almonds and demerara (raw) sugar. Peel, core and chop the apples. Mix the apples and drained cherries.

Preheat the oven to 200 C / 400 F / Gas 6.

Brush a baking tray (sheet) with some of the melted butter. Lay down one sheet of filo, brush with melted butter and sprinkle with about a teaspoon of the sugar/almond mix. Cover with another sheet of filo. Repeat until you have used up all the filo.

Sprinkle over the remaining sugar/almond mix. Cover with the apples and cherries. Drizzle with about a tablespoon of reserved juice. Roll up lengthwise to form a long sausage.

Brush the filo top with melted butter and sprinkle with a teaspoon of demerara (raw) sugar. Bake for 25 minutes or until crisp and golden. Rest for 5 minutes before slicing and serving.

Mix a little of the remaining juice with the cornflower. Stir into the rest, place it all in a small saucepan and heat gently, stirring until thick and glossy.

Serve slices of strudel with whipped cream drizzled with thickened syrup.

Autumn Pork Pie

Pork pies are a fabulous picnic food, a great addition to a buffet table, or just an impressive cook ahead centrepiece for lunch or supper. People worry about hot water crust pastry, but trust us, it is very easy to make and indeed much more forgiving than other pastries. The use of gently spiced mulberry syrup in the jelly gives a rich colour and a warm autumnal flavour to the pie, making it perfect fare during or after a bracing autumn walk. The spiced jelly is like serving the pie with its own chutney, but if you like serve it with our Cherry Ginger Chutney (page 110).

Serves 6

Pastry
400 g / 14 oz / 3 ½ cups plain (all purpose) flour
150 g / 5 oz lard
175 ml / 6 fl oz / ¾ cup water

Filling
400 g / 14 oz pork mince (ground pork)
250 g / 8 oz pork shoulder, finely diced
150 g / 5 oz streaky bacon
½ teaspoon grated nutmeg
1 teaspoon chopped thyme leaves
½ teaspoon salt

Jelly
3 leaves gelatine
100 ml / 3 ½ fl oz / ⅓ mulberry syrup
60 ml / 2 fl oz / ¼ cup water
½ teaspoon ground cloves
½ teaspoon ground cinnamon

Heat the oven to 190 C / 375 F / Gas 5. Then mix together all the ingredients for the filling in a bowl. Season well and set aside.

Put the lard and water in a small saucepan and heat to melt the lard. Bring up to boiling point. Sift the flour into a bowl, pour the lard and water mix into the flour and stir to combine. Cool slightly. When cool enough to handle (but not cold), knead to a pliable dough. Break off a quarter of the dough and reserve for the lid. Roll out the rest of the dough and line a 20 cm / 8 inch springform tin.

Fill the pastry case with the meat filling. Roll out the last piece of pastry to make a lid. Brush the top rim of the pastry with cold water, fit on the lid and crimp around the edges, pinching the pastry between thumb and forefinger to form a small pleat (this is not essential but is traditional and looks pretty so we encourage you to give it a go). Cut a cross in the middle of the pie to let the steam escape.

Put into the oven and cook for 30 minutes. Remove the pie from the oven and brush with beaten egg. Turn the oven down to 160 C / 325 F / Gas 3. Cook a further hour. Remove from the oven and let it cool.

Soak the gelatine leaves in water for 5 minutes until pliable.

Remove and squeeze out the excess water. Bring the mulberry syrup, water and spices to the boil and remove from the heat. Add the gelatine leaves and stir to dissolve. Cool to room temperature. Using a small funnel gradually pour the gelatine syrup into the pie. This is the hardest bit (but not too hard), work slowly to avoid flooding the pie. Start by putting the funnel in the centre steam gap, then make some small slits around the outside. Pour the syrup in gently. Return to the fridge for a couple of hours to set completely.

Serve cut in large wedges with salad.

Mulberry Bakewell Pie

This is a glorious mash-up, where Bakewell Tart meets Berry Pie. We like to serve this as a dessert with clotted cream. If you like you can substitute the berry filling for a thick layer of mulberry jam; in this case you won't need the ground almonds sprinkled on the base, the function of which is to soak up some of the juice from the mulberries. The jam version is in fact better if you are planning on eating the pie over several days, as the super juicy mulberries can result (even with the ground almonds) in a soggy bottom experience if kept in the fridge. It will still taste good but the pastry base will absorb all the juice making it soft and pink.

The use of vodka in making pastry (pie crust) may seem odd, but trust us on this. Water activates the gluten in flour and can make the pastry tough, whilst vodka provides the liquid necessary to bind the pastry without toughening it. But by all means, if you prefer or don't have a bottle of vodka to hand, just use a little water.

Serves 6-8

For the pastry case
150 g / 5 oz / 1 ¼ cups plain (all purpose) flour
75 g / 2 ½ oz / 5 tablespoons butter
1 tablespoon caster sugar
1 egg yolk

1 tablespoon of vodka or water if required
1 tablespoon ground almonds

For the filling
400 g / 14 oz / 2 cups fresh or frozen (defrosted) mulberries
2 tablespoons of honey
2 tablespoons ground almonds
1 tablespoon cornflour (cornstarch)

For the topping
150 g / 5 oz / 1 ⅓ sticks butter
150 g / 5 oz / ⅔ cup caster (superfine) sugar
150 g / 5 oz / 1 ½ cups ground almonds
4 eggs

For the glaze
¼ cup icing (confectioners') sugar
1 tablespoon mulberry syrup or (better) mulberry gin

Preheat the oven to 180 C / 350 F / Gas 4.

Put the butter, sugar and flour in a food processor and whizz to fine crumbs (if making by hand rub the butter into the flour and sugar until the mixture resembles fine crumbs). Add the egg and mix briefly. If required, add enough vodka or cold water to form a dough. Wrap in cling film (saran wrap) and rest in the fridge for at least half an hour.

Roll out the pastry and use to line a 20 cm / 8 inch pie dish. Line with baking paper, fill with baking beans and bake the case blind for 15 minutes. Remove the baking beans and paper and bake for another 5 minutes to dry out the base. Sprinkle the base with the ground almonds.

Put the mulberries in a bowl. In a separate small bowl, mix together the honey and cornflour (cornstarch), then stir into the mulberries. Pour this into the pastry case.

Cream the butter and sugar until light and fluffy. Add the ground almonds and egg and mix together. Spoon over the fruit and bake for

40-45 minutes until golden brown and a skewer inserted in the topping comes out clean (remember you have fruit under that topping, you are looking for a skewer clean of uncooked cake batter). Leave to cool.

Sift the icing sugar. Add the syrup or gin, gradually stirring well to form a smooth pourable consistency. Drizzle over the pie in a random pattern.

Sausage Rolls

These only came about because we asked our tasters what they'd like and one said 'sausage rolls'. Our immediate response was 'No, this is a book on cherries', but then we realised the potential for a truly delicious roll, with the tartness of the fruit balancing the richness of the meat. If you can find venison sausage meat it is amazing. Venison mince is also delicious, but they become Game Rolls as the texture makes a great difference.

If you close up the ends these become the so-popular-at-the-moment hand pies. Hand pies originated in the Southern states of America and here the marriage with a so-British game roll is truly a match made in heaven.

Makes 8 short fat rolls

450 g / 15 oz sausage meat
handful dried cherries, chopped (20-25 g / ¾-1 oz or more if you want your rolls very fruity)
6-8 leaves fresh sage, finely torn
1 sheet frozen puff pastry, defrosted (sheets are best as they have nice straight edges)
1 egg, beaten

Preheat the oven to 220 C / 425 F / Gas 7.

Put the sausage meat, dried cherries and sage in a bowl and mix well. The cherries will tend to want to stick together in a lump; don't let them.

On a lightly floured surface unroll the pastry sheet and cut in half lengthwise. Roll it gently both ways so it is a little thinner. This gives a good pastry/filling balance. If you are using a block of pastry you will probably only need half. Roll it so it makes two long strips 11 cm / 4 ½ inch by 30 cm / 12 inch, and about 2 mm / $^1/_{10}$ inch thick (i.e. thin but not falling into holes).

Divide the filling into two portions and place one on each strip of pastry. Squish (yes, this is a culinary term) into long sausage shapes so they stretch the length of the pastry. Cut each strip into four and roll up to make the individual sausage rolls. Seal each with a little beaten egg. Place the rolls on a lightly-greased baking tray (baking sheet), with the joins face-down. Brush the tops lightly with egg and make a couple of diagonal cuts on each one.

Bake for 20-25 minutes until golden. Eat immediately or transfer to a wire tray to cool.

CHERRY CHOCOLATE GINGER TART

Cherry, chocolate and ginger: this is all your favourite chocolates (candies) in dessert form. The dark chocolate and ginger make it a sophisticated dessert to serve at a dinner party.

Serves 8-10

200 g / 7 oz gingernuts (ginger cookies)
150 g / 5 oz digestive biscuits
150 g / 5 oz / 1 ⅓ sticks butter
625 g / 1 lb 4 oz fresh cherries or a large jar of morello cherries drained
1 teaspoon cornflour (cornstarch)
250 ml / 8 fl oz / 1 cup good quality cherry jam
100 g / 3 ½ oz dark (bittersweet) chocolate, chopped
300 ml / 10 fl oz / 1 ¼ cups double (heavy) cream
¼ cup ginger in syrup, drained and chopped
extra dark (bittersweet) chocolate and extra whole cherries to decorate

Melt the butter. Put the gingernut and digestive biscuits (cookies) into the food processor and whizz to form fine crumbs. If you don't have a food processor put the biscuits into a plastic bag and bash with a rolling pin to form crumbs (very therapeutic). Mix in the melted butter and press into a loose bottomed 20 cm / 8 inch tin to form a base. Chill for at least 30 minutes.

If you are using fresh cherries, stone them, if you are using frozen cherries defrost completely. Mix the cornflour into the jam and put it in a pan over a low heat. Cook, stirring, for 2-3 minutes until thick. Remove from the heat and stir in the cherries. Allow to cool then pour into the tart shell. Put in the fridge for at least an hour to set.

Put the chopped chocolate into a heatproof bowl. Heat a third of the cream in a small saucepan and when it reaches boiling point pour over the chocolate and stir until the chocolate melts. Allow it to cool slightly. Whisk the remaining cream to soft peaks and fold it and the ginger into the chocolate mix. Spread over the cherries and set aside until ready to serve. Grate the last measure of chocolate over the top and decorate with whole cherries.

Cherry and Almond Tart

The joy of this tart is that you can serve it hot, warm or cold. It is sufficiently robust to take on picnics and looks good enough to grace a dinner table. It can be made with fresh or tinned cherries so you can have it all year round. Oh, and it is totally delicious.

Serves 6 to 8

Pastry
250 g / 8 oz / 2 cups plain (all purpose) flour
pinch salt
1 tablespoon caster sugar
150 g / 5 oz / 1 ⅓ sticks cold butter, cut into small chunks
1 egg yolk, mixed with a little cold water so it can be poured easily

Filling

100 g / 3 ½ oz / 7 tablespoons butter, softened
100 g / 3 ½ oz / ½ cup caster (superfine) sugar
½ teaspoon almond extract
2 eggs, lightly beaten
30 g / 1 ¼ oz / 2 tablespoons plain (all purpose) flour
135 g / 4 ¾ oz / 1 ⅛ cups ground almonds
500 g / 1 lb fresh cherries, stoned or 2 tins of black cherries, drained
1 tablespoon kirsch

Topping

1 tablespoon caster (superfine) sugar (this is only if you are going
to serve the tart hot, as it gives it a lovely crunchy topping)

The pastry is taken from Sarah Raven's *Garden Cookbook*; it is slightly sweet and remains crisp and crumbly under the filling. Put the flour, salt and sugar into a food processor and give a quick blitz to ensure there are no lumps. Add the butter and mix until it resembles fine breadcrumbs. With the machine running add the egg mixture a little at a time until the pastry just holds together. Be careful not to add too much water. Wrap the dough in cling film (saran wrap) and put in the fridge for 30 minutes.

Preheat the oven to 190 C / 375 F / Gas 5. Lightly grease a 23 cm / 9 inch tart tin. On a lightly floured surface roll out the pastry so it lines the base and sides of the tin. The pastry is very crumbly and will fall apart but it doesn't matter; just patch it up, smoothing the joins with a damp finger. The edges look fine rough and uneven. Prick the base with a fork and cover with baking paper and baking beans. Blind bake for 12-15 minutes. Remove the beans and paper and leave to cool.

Turn the oven to 200 C / 400 F / Gas 6.

Set aside 2 tablespoons of ground almonds. Beat the butter, sugar and almond extract together in a bowl. Add the eggs, flour, ground almonds and kirsch and mix gently. Sprinkle the remaining ground almonds over the base of the pastry case. Cut the cherries in half and pat them dry with kitchen paper (this is particularly important if you are using tinned cherries). Spread about ⅔ of the cherries onto the ground almonds. Dollop the almond mixture on top and spread so it is even. Put the rest of the cherries on top, cut face down. If you intend to serve the tart hot, sprinkle a spoonful of caster sugar over the top.

Bake for 40 minutes. Leave to cool for a few moments and then transfer to a pretty serving plate. Serve with lots of thick or clotted cream or crème fraiche.

Quick Cherry Tarte Tatin

Tarte tatin is often made with apples or pears, but there are a myriad of different versions available, including some lovely savoury versions, so we thought why not a cherry tarte tatin? It was a happy thought and this is the delicious result. One of the great attractions is that despite the sophisticated name it really is tremendously easy to make – particularly if you use bought puff pastry sheets and employ this trick of using honey instead of making caramel. And why wouldn't you? We can make puff pastry, but let's be honest no one ever does, as the all-butter versions you can buy are really very good.

Serves 4
60 g / 2 oz / ¼ cup honey
1 vanilla pod
15 g / ½ oz / 1 tablespoon butter
200 g / 7 oz / 2 cups fresh cherries (or frozen cherries defrosted and drained)
1 sheet puff pastry

Take a 20 cm / 8 inch cast-iron frying pan (skillet) and use it as a guide to cut a circle from the pastry sheet about 2.5 cm / 1 inch wider than the pan.

Put the honey into the frying pan (skillet) and scrape in the seeds from the vanilla pod. Heat gently and cook for about 10 minutes until sticky. Remove from the heat, stir in the butter, add the cherries and stir to coat.

Lay the pastry over the cherries and tuck down the edges. Put into the oven and cook for around 30 minutes until the pastry is puffed and golden. Leave to sit for 5-10 minutes then turn out. Serve with whipped cream.

Lattice Cherry Pie

This is a very pretty pie with the deep red fruit showing through the crisp lattice topping. It is equally delicious warm or cold. Our pie dish is 20 cm / 8 inches across and 2.5 cm / 1 inch deep but a little larger or smaller wouldn't matter. A fluted rim gives a pretty finish; you need to bring this pie to the table in the dish as it tends to fall apart when you serve it. If you have one of those fancy lattice cutters (Sally does, but then there are few kitchen gadgets that don't lurk somewhere in her kitchen cupboards) by all means use this.

Serves 4-6

Pastry
200 g / 7 oz / 1 ³/₅ cups plain (all purpose) flour
100 g / 3 ½ oz / 7 tablespoons butter, chilled and cut into chunks
1 egg, beaten
cold water to bind

Filling
640 g / 1 lb 5 oz / 3 cups cherries, pitted fresh or tinned
2 tablespoons kirsch
110 g / 4 oz / ½ cup caster (superfine) sugar (taste your cherries; you may need less)
2 teaspoons cornflower (cornstarch)
1 egg, beaten, to glaze

Put the cherries into a bowl with the caster (superfine) sugar and kirsch. Leave for an hour or so.

You can make the pastry either in a food processor or by hand. If you are making it by hand, rub the butter lightly into the flour until the mixture forms dry crumbs, then cut in the egg with a knife, working quickly to combine. If necessary, add a little cold water until the mixture just holds together. If you are using a food processor, pulse the flour and butter until the mixture forms crumbs. Add the egg and pulse until the mixture comes together, adding a little cold water if necessary. Wrap the pastry in cling film (saran wrap) and put into the fridge for at least 30 minutes to rest.

Preheat the oven to 200 C / 400 F / Gas 6. Pour off the juice from the cherries into a small saucepan. Separately mix a little with a teaspoon of the cornflower (cornstarch) to make a runny paste. Add this to the saucepan, bring to the boil and simmer for a couple of minutes, stirring until thick and glossy. If the sauce is still thin, add the rest of the cornflower (cornstarch), repeating the above procedure.

Divide the pastry into roughly two-thirds and one-third. Roll out the larger piece for the base of the pie and drop into the pie dish. Roll out the second piece of pastry and cut into 12-14 strips. It is easiest to do this on a sheet of baking paper. Roughly draw a circle the size of your pie dish. Lay out half the strips going one way and then weave the remaining strips in and out to form the lattice.

Put the cherries and thickened juice into the pie dish and flip the lattice on top. This is easier said than done and some of the strips will fall out of place but it is easy to realign them. Press the edges together firmly using your fingers or the tines of a fork, and brush with beaten egg.

Bake for about 25 minutes until the top is golden brown. Allow to sit for about 10-15 minutes. Serve warm or at room temperature with lots of thick cream or custard.

DESSERTS AND PUDDINGS

CHERRY JUBILEE

This classic dessert was reputedly created by Auguste Escoffier to commemorate Queen Victoria's Diamond Jubilee in 1897. Traditionally this is served in individual silver cups. If, however, your royal plate hasn't been polished recently, feel free to use individual china ramekins.

Serves 6

150 g / 5 oz / ⅔ cup sugar
zest of half a lemon
500 g / 1 lb / 2 ½ cups cherries, pitted
1 tablespoon arrowroot or cornflour (cornstarch)
4-5 tablespoons kirsch

Make a simple sugar syrup by putting the sugar in a heavy-bottomed saucepan, adding 300 ml / ½ pint / 1 ¼ cups of water and the lemon zest. Bring to a simmer and stir until the sugar has completely dissolved. Add the cherries and poach gently for 5 minutes. Remove the cherries and set aside. Increase the heat and boil hard to reduce the syrup volume by half.

Mix the arrowroot to a smooth paste with 1 tablespoon of water. Stir into the reduced cherry liquid. Heat gently, stirring until it has thickened. Remove from the heat and return the cherries to the pan.

Divide between 6 ramekins. Take to the table to serve. Pour the kirsch over the cherries and flambé. Serve with cream or ice cream.

SUMMER PUDDING

Summer pudding is delicious with any combination of berries but it is particularly good made with either just mulberries or a mixture of mulberries and other berries. The delicate flavour, rich colour and extreme juiciness of the mulberries raise this from being a mere pudding into a sublime dessert.

Serves 6 depending on greed.

850 g / 2 lb / 5 cups mulberries or mixed berries (avoid strawberries as they tend to go mushy)
150 g / 5 oz / ⅔ cup caster sugar, to taste
7-8 slices day-old, white bread, crusts removed

You will need a 900 ml / 1 ¾ pint pudding basin, lightly buttered (your pudding basin's capacity in mls should be about the same as the amount of fruit in grams). Put the fruit and sugar into a large saucepan and heat gently until the sugar just melts. Remove from the heat and set aside.

Line the pudding basin with the bread, ensuring there are no gaps. Reserve ⅔ of the cup of juice and then pour the remaining juice and fruit into the bread-lined bowl.

Cover the top with a slice of bread, cut to fit the bowl, and press down well. Place a small plate on top and put a heavy weight on top of it. Leave in the fridge overnight.

Loosen with a knife and turn onto a deep platter, spooning the remaining juice over any white bits. Serve with lots of cream.

CHOCOLATE CHERRY CHRISTMAS PUDDING

This is the ultimate Christmas pudding and will instantly convert even those who claim not to like the traditional version. It's chocolatey, fruity, rich and laced with booze, there is nothing not to like. You can make it up and cook it up to two months ahead, and just reheat on the day, or make up to the point of cooking it on Christmas Eve and let it steam away on Christmas Day. We owe this recipe to Jane Hornby who created it for *BBC Good Food Magazine*. We swopped dried cherries for her sultanas and tweaked the method very slightly as neither of us owns a microwave, but otherwise it is all hers, as you can't improve on perfection.

Serves 10 (possibly more if they are stuffed full of turkey)

200 g / 7 oz frozen dark sweet cherries, defrosted
1 conference pear

100 g / 3 ½ oz raisins
100 g / 3 ½ oz dried cherries
100 ml / 3 ½ fl oz / ⅓ cherry brandy
100 g / 3 ½ oz dark (bittersweet) chocolate
100 g / 3 ½ oz / 7 tablespoons butter plus extra for greasing
2 eggs
50 g / 1 ½ oz / ²/₅ cup plain (all purpose) flour
100 g / 3 ½ oz / ½ cup dark soft brown sugar
1 teaspoon mixed spice
1 tablespoon cocoa powder
50 g / 1 ½ oz fresh breadcrumbs

For the sauce
100 g / 3 ½ oz dark (bittersweet) chocolate
125 ml / 4 fl oz / ½ cup double (heavy) cream
2 tablespoons golden (corn) syrup
3 tablespoons brandy

Drain and halve the cherries. Peel and grate the pear. In a large heavy-bottomed saucepan mix the cherries, pear, brandy and dried fruit. Bring to the boil, then turn off the heat.

Break up the chocolate and dice the butter, add to the fruit mix and stir to melt. Leave to cool.

Sift together the flour, spices and cocoa powder and stir this, together with the brown sugar, into the fruit mixture. Beat the eggs and stir these, and a good pinch of salt and the breadcrumbs, into the mixture.

Place in a greased 1 litre / 1 ¾ pint pudding basin. Cut two large squares of aluminium foil and grease one side of one square. Put them together, buttered side outmost and fold to make a pleat in the middle to allow for expansion, as the pudding swells as it cooks. Place over the pudding basin, buttered side down and tie tightly round the basin.

Take a large saucepan, big enough to hold the pudding basin, and put an upturned saucer in the bottom as a trivet. Place the pudding basin on the saucer. Boil a kettle and pour enough water to come halfway up the pudding basin in the saucepan. Place on the heat. Cover the pan and steam the pudding for two and a half hours. Check every now and then to make sure the water level has not dropped too low and top up as necessary. Check that a skewer comes out clean. If you are making this ahead of time, allow it to cool completely and store in a cool dark place for up to two months.

To reheat, steam for 30 minutes or reheat for 5 minutes in a microwave. To make the sauce, bring some water to the boil in a large saucepan or the bottom half of a bain-marie and remove from the heat. Put all the ingredients in a metal bowl or the top half of the bain-marie and stir gently till melted. Pour over the slices of pudding.

Mulberry Sorbet

A light refreshing sorbet, perfect for a summer dessert. Layered up with thick Greek yoghurt, drizzled with a little honey and sprinkled with chopped pistachios, this makes a beautiful sundae.

400 g / 14 oz / 2 cups fresh or frozen (defrosted) mulberries
315 g / 10 ½ oz / 1 ½ cups caster (superfine) sugar
375 ml / 13 fl oz / 1 ½ cups water
2 tablespoons mulberry liqueur (see page 113) or crème de cassis

Put the sugar and water in a saucepan and stir over a low heat to dissolve the sugar. Whizz the mulberries in a food processor. Sieve to remove any stalks and stir the resulting juice and the liqueur into the sugar syrup. Cool.

Churn in an ice cream maker following the machine instructions, or place in a rigid container in the freezer and freeze till hard, breaking the ice crystals up with a fork every couple of hours.

Clafoutis

This is a wonderful pudding but it is messy to serve, so make it in a pretty dish that you can bring to the table. That way everyone can admire it before you dollop it onto their plates.

Serves 4-5

50 g / 1 ¾ oz / ⅓ stick unsalted butter
4 eggs
125 g / 4 oz / ½ cup caster (superfine) sugar
50 g / 1 ¾ oz / ²⁄₅ cup plain flour
250 ml / 8 fl oz / 1 cup milk
1 teaspoon vanilla extract
450 g / 15 oz sweet cherries, destalked and pitted if you wish.
Out of season, tinned cherries are okay but need to be drained
very well.
icing (confectioners') sugar

Heat the oven to 190 C / 375 F / Gas 5.

Melt the butter in a small pan. Whisk the eggs in a big bowl using an electric hand mixer, this will give you a better batter than in a processor. Add the sugar, then the flour, then the butter and finally the milk and vanilla extract, whisking each one in well.

Lightly butter a 23 cm / 9 inch dish. The base needs to be completely flat and the batter will cook more evenly if the sides are straight. Spread the cherries over the base of the dish and pour in the batter.

Bake for about 40 minutes until golden brown and just setting.
Sprinkle with icing sugar and serve warm.

Mulberry Labneh with Candied Nuts and Seeds

Serves 4

250 ml / 8 fl oz / 1 cup unsweetened natural yoghurt
pinch of salt
400 g / 14 oz mulberries
1 ½ teaspoons caster (superfine) sugar

3 tablespoons runny honey
2 teaspoons rose water
250 ml / 8 fl oz / 1 cup crème fraiche
2 tablespoons pistachio nuts, chopped
2 tablespoons pumpkin seeds

Mix together the yoghurt and salt and stir well. Line a sieve with muslin or a clean J cloth and sit it over a large bowl. Put the yoghurt mix into the sieve and leave for 4 hours to drain. Stir the crème fraiche into the labneh.

Whizz half the mulberries with the rose water and fold through the labneh to make a ripple. Place the remaining mulberries in 4 glass bowls and top with the rippled yoghurt.

Heat a heavy-bottomed frying (sauté) pan. Add the seeds, nuts and honey and cook gently, stirring to coat the nuts and seeds with honey. Cook till the honey turns a golden caramelized colour and put onto a sheet of greaseproof paper and leave to set. Once the nuts are set, sprinkle over the top of the labneh and serve immediately.

BLACK FOREST ALASKA

This is a magnificent cultural car crash: American ice cream meets German cake in a wonderful dessert. You can make one large one but it is hard to slice with any elegance so we prefer to make individual cup-cake-size Alaskas. The key is to make sure the ice cream is frozen hard and completely covered by the meringue to avoid puddle disasters.

This makes 6 Alaskas but you get a tray of 12 cake bases (it's pointless trying to make fewer). You can keep extra ice cream toppings frozen and the cake bases in a tin and just make them up to order over the week or just make up ice cream and meringue for the number you need and top the other cake bases with fresh cherry butter cream (see the recipe for Cherry Sandwich Cake, page 149-50).

You can use vanilla ice cream but we think this is a bit sweet and prefer the contrast of bitter chocolate.

Serves 6

125 g / 4 oz / 1 stick butter
125 g / 4 oz / ½ cup golden caster (superfine) sugar
2 eggs
1 tablespoon golden (corn) syrup
125 g / 4 oz / 1 ⅓ cups self-raising flour
1 teaspoon baking powder
2 tablespoons cocoa powder
125 g / 4 oz / ½ cup black cherry conserve
1 tablespoon cherry brandy
6 egg whites
450 g / 16 oz / 3 ½ cups golden caster (superfine) sugar
500 g / 1 pint / 2 cups bitter chocolate ice cream
2 tablespoon plain (bittersweet) chocolate, grated

Preheat the oven to 170 C / 325 F / Gas 3. Grease and line a twelve-hole cupcake tray.

Cream the butter and sugar till light and fluffy. Add the eggs one at a time beating after each addition. Beat in golden (corn) syrup. Sift together the flour and baking powder and fold into the batter.

Divide the mixture between the cake cases. For Alaska bases you want a cake a little lower than a cupcake, so only fill those cases half full. Fill any you are going to use as cupcakes three-quarter full. Bake for 15-20 minutes or until a skewer inserted into the centre of the cake comes out clean. Let cool in the tin for 10 minutes then remove from the tray to cool completely on a rack.

Remove the ice cream from the freezer and line six of the holes in the cupcake tin with cling film (saran wrap) and fill with chocolate ice cream. Return to the freezer and freeze hard.

Mix the cherry conserve with the cherry brandy.

When ready to serve, preheat the oven to 220 C / 425 F / Gas 7.

Remove 6 bases from the cupcake tray. Trim if necessary to give a flat base and place 6 bases on a baking tray (sheet). Cover each base with a thick layer of cherry conserve.

Whisk the egg whites to stiff peaks and gradually add the sugar,

CHERRIES & MULBERRIES

whisking constantly until the meringue is thick and glossy.

Using the cling film (saran wrap) to remove the ice cream from the cake tin, peel away the film and place a disc of ice cream on each base. Cover completely with meringue using a knife or spatula.

Put them into the oven. Bake for 3-4 minutes or until the meringues are firm and the tips of the meringue are just turning brown. Remove to serving plates using a fish slice or spatula. Sprinkle with grated chocolate and serve immediately.

CONFECTIONERY

CHERRY RIPE BITES

After our success with home-made walnut whips (see *Nuts: Growing and Cooking* for the recipe) we were emboldened to recreate another childhood confectionery treat. Cherry Ripes are an Antipodean sweet, a chocolate-covered cherry coconut bar (think of the bastard child of coconut ice and a Bounty bar with a touch of cherry). Tremendously popular down under, this is Australia's oldest chocolate bar. Making them will make any homesick Aussies very happy. Our version uses dark chocolate and a biscuit base, and is quite rich so cut them small.

Makes 16 pieces

150 g / 5 oz / 1 ¼ sticks butter
150 g / 5 oz / 1 ¼ cups plain (all purpose) flour
60 g / 2 ½ oz / ½ cups cornflour (cornstarch)
60 g / 2 ½ oz / ⅔ cups icing (confectioners') sugar
15 g / 1 oz cocoa powder
270 g / 9 oz / 3 cups desiccated coconut
60 ml / 2 fl oz / ¼ cup maple syrup
60 ml / ¼ cup virgin coconut oil
300 g / 10 oz glacé cherries
200 g / 6 oz dark (bittersweet) chocolate

1 tablespoon golden (corn) syrup
15 g / ½ oz / 1 tablespoon butter

Preheat oven 180 C / 350 F / Gas 4. Line a 20 x 25 cm / 8 x 10 inch baking tray at least 5 cm / 2 inch deep.

Melt the butter. Sift together the flour, cornflour (cornstarch), icing sugar and cocoa powder. Stir in the melted butter and mix to a soft dough. Press into a lined tray and bake for 20-25 minutes until the base is cooked. The cocoa powder means the dough will not colour, so touch it – you are looking for a dry sandy texture. Remove the tray from the oven and cool completely.

Put half the glacé cherries, coconut, maple syrup and coconut oil in the food processor and blend for a few minutes, scraping down the edges of the bowl. You want the mixture to be well blended. Cut the remaining cherries in half (or quarters if really large) and stir into the coconut mixture. Press the coconut mixture firmly down onto the base and chill in the fridge for an hour or until set.

Bring some water to the boil in a large saucepan or the bottom of a bain-marie and remove from the heat. Place the chocolate, remaining butter and golden syrup into a bowl or top half of a bain-marie over the water to melt. Stir to combine and when completely melted pour over the coconut layer and leave somewhere cool to set. Cut into squares.

CHERRY FUDGE

This makes delicious crumbly fudge similar to Scottish tablet. In theory, it keeps well in a tin but ours has always been eaten before we can test that part of the recipe. It is based on a recipe in *The Cook's Scrapbook*, published by the Reader's Digest in 1995. Quite apart from having lots of good recipes, this book is filled with charming pictures of a bygone age: the countryside was always magically misty, little fishing boats chugged in and out of pretty harbours, and everyone ate by candlelight. Not a car, iPad or piece of plastic in sight.

Makes 36 pieces

200 g / 7 oz glacé cherries or 150 g / 5 oz dried cherries
115 g / 4 oz / 1 stick butter
550 g / 19 ½ oz / 2 ¾ cups caster (superfine) sugar
4 tablespoons water
2 tablespoons golden (corn) syrup
175 ml / 6 fl oz / ¾ cup condensed milk
½ teaspoon vanilla extract

Line an 18 cm / 7 inch shallow tin with baking paper.

Chop the cherries reasonably finely. It is best to use either glacé or dried rather than a mixture. Our testers preferred glacé but by a narrow margin.

Put the water, butter, sugar and syrup into a heavy-bottomed saucepan and stir over a low heat until the sugar is dissolved and everything is well mixed. Brush the sides of the pan periodically to ensure the sugar doesn't lurk there undissolved.

Add the condensed milk and bring to the boil, stirring all the time. Cook slowly for about 10 minutes until the temperature reaches 118 C / 240 F on a sugar thermometer. If you don't have a sugar thermometer, remove the pan from the heat and drop a small amount of the mixture into a bowl of cold water. If you can form it into a soft ball, it's ready. If not, continue cooking and test again, removing the pan from the heat each time. Once the mixture is ready, remove the pan from the heat and allow the bubbles to subside. Add the vanilla extract and beat with a wooden spoon until the fudge is thick and creamy; it will set a little more as it cools. Stir in the cherries, pour into the tin and leave to cool.

Just before the fudge is fully set, mark the squares with a sharp knife. Cut when it is completely cold. Store in a tin if it doesn't all disappear at once.

Cherry Truffles

With a little imagination, these look exactly like real cherries. More to the point, they are utterly delicious. If you want very red cherries, the amount of colouring needed may mean the chocolate does not fully set; in which case serve the truffles in dainty paper cases. This recipe contains uncooked egg yolk so be sure to advise people of this.

Makes about 25 cherries

50 g / 1 ¾ oz / ¼ cup dried cherries, chopped
2 tablespoons kirsch
30 g / 1 oz / 1 ½ tablespoon butter
30 ml / 1 fl oz / 1 tablespoon double (heavy) cream
125 g / 4 oz dark (bittersweet) chocolate
1 small egg yolk
cocoa powder, to roll
175 g / 6 oz white chocolate for dipping
red paste food colouring
10 orange Matchmakers

Put the cherries in the kirsch and leave to soak for at least one hour.

Bring a saucepan of water to the boil and remove from the heat. Put the first measure of chocolate, butter and cream in a heatproof bowl or a bain-marie and place over the hot water and leave to melt. Stir occasionally, add the egg yolk, fruit and soaking liquor and stir to combine. Put into the fridge and chill until set (about a couple of hours).

Dust your hands in cocoa and gently form into small balls (about the size of a large cherry). Break the Matchmakers into thirds and, using a skewer to make the hole, insert the 'stalk' into each truffle. Return to the fridge to chill for half an hour.

Melt the white chocolate over hot water as before. When it has melted, remove from the heat and add the food colouring a blob at a time, mixing well until you get the colour you want. Use the most concentrated paste colouring you can find; you need quite a lot of colour to make the chocolate a good 'cherry red' and liquid colouring will make the chocolate too runny. If the chocolate starts to set, simply add a little cold water (a few drops at a time) and beat until smooth and runny again.

Holding the stalk, coat each truffle in the chocolate. Place on a sheet of greaseproof paper and put in the fridge to set. Some of the chocolate will drip down but you can trim this when the cherries are set. If necessary put the truffles into little paper cases. They will keep for several days in the fridge.

AFTER DINNER PYRAMIDS

These chocolates are a huge improvement (we think) on after dinner mints, even if they are a little richer. You can easily buy silicone trays of little pyramid moulds from specialist cook shops or online. Mini muffin cases would also work. Our testers couldn't decide whether they preferred marzipan or fondant and were about to come to blows over the matter, so we have included both variations.

Makes 15 chocolates

110 g / 3 ¾ oz dark (bittersweet) chocolate
100 g / 3 ½ oz white marzipan OR 110 g / 3 ¾ oz ready-made fondant icing
1 tablespoon cherry curd (shop-bought or see page 118)
2 teaspoons kirsch

Set a large pan of water or the bottom half of a bain-marie on a high heat, bring to the boil and turn off the heat. Immediately place the chocolate, broken into pieces, into the top half of the bain-marie or a heatproof bowl over the water and leave to melt.

Oil the moulds. Take a pastry brush and brush the insides of the moulds liberally with melted chocolate. Place them in the fridge for 10 minutes to harden, keeping the chocolate over the water. When the chocolate is hard, apply a second layer to give a shell which completely coats the inside of the moulds. Pop this back in the fridge to set. Keep the remaining chocolate as you will need it for the base of the pyramids.

Roll out the marzipan or fondant so it is about ½ cm / ¼ inch thick. Remember to use icing sugar not flour to coat the worktop and rolling pin. Cut little circles and push them into the moulds. You want the marzipan/fondant to cover the inside and reach about halfway up the sides (you need room for the sealing layer of marzipan/fondant and a layer of chocolate which will form the base of the pyramid). Put a small blob of curd into each pyramid. Seal gently with a layer of marzipan/fondant, being careful not to let the curd ooze out.

Brush the base with melted chocolate and return to the fridge to set. Repeat if necessary. Turn the pyramids out onto a plate and trim away any rough edges. These chocolates are best eaten straight from the fridge. In the unlikely event that they aren't all eaten, they will keep in the fridge for a couple of days.

Toffee Cherries

Think toffee apples but with cherries. Now isn't that a lovely thought. These are lovely to serve after dinner as a petit four or to use to decorate cakes and desserts. You should warn guests that the stone is still in there to avoid expensive dental disasters (we know health and safety cautions to stone them, but to keep the shape and serve them on the stem you really need to keep them whole).

Makes about a dozen

12 firm cherries on the stem
100 g / 3 ½ oz caster sugar
¼ teaspoon white vinegar
1 tablespoon golden (corn) syrup

Boil a kettle. Put the cherries in a large bowl and pour over the boiling water. Drain and dry thoroughly with kitchen paper. This step removes any waxy coating and ensures that the toffee sticks. Lay out a sheet of non-stick baking paper or a silicon baking mat.

Put the sugar into a saucepan with two tablespoons of water and heat gently over a medium heat until the sugar dissolves. Try to avoid the temptation to stir the pan, just swirl it, this will reduce the risk of the sugar crystallizing. Stir in the vinegar and syrup. Increase the heat and cook until the syrup turns a light caramel colour and a small drop placed in a cup of cold water hardens. If you use a sugar thermometer, this is 150 C / 300 F or the hard crack stage, however we find it difficult to use a thermometer for this kind of small quantity.

Holding the cherries by the stalk, swirl them through the caramel until well covered. Place on the baking paper to set. In theory, these will keep up to two days in a cool dry place but we find it best to make them just a few hours ahead.

Toot

This delightfully named confectionery is a traditional Persian sweet – a mix of ground almonds and sugar shaped to look like a mulberry. It is also sometimes called *tut* and the name comes from the Persian word for the mulberry fruit. Black mulberry is called *shah toot* (or king mulberry). The oval-shaped sweets (there is some artistic license in seeing these as mulberries particularly if you don't use food colouring) are traditionally served at Persian New Year.

Makes 12-15

125 g / 4 oz / 1 cup ground almonds
90 g / 3 oz / ¾ cup icing (confectioners') sugar
½ teaspoon ground cardamom
1 ½ tablespoons rosewater or mulberry juice
purple food colouring (optional)
60 g / 2 oz / ¼ cup granulated sugar
slivered pistachios

Combine ground almonds, icing sugar and cardamom. Gradually add the rosewater or mulberry juice and a few drops of food colouring if using and knead to a soft paste. Set aside for half an hour or so to firm up. Form into mulberry shapes and roll in the granulated sugar. Add a slivered pistachio into the long end as a stalk. Serve on a pretty plate.

CAKES AND BAKING

CHERRY CAKE

Cherry cake is a must-bake for a traditional afternoon tea table. The perennial problem with cherry cake is the cherries sinking to the bottom. You can minimize this by tossing the cherries in flour and by adding a third of them at the end, but it is to some extent inevitable and we have found it best to just embrace a thick level of bottom dwelling cherries as part of the charm of the cake. You can make this in a ring or Bundt tin (Mary Berry does), but we prefer to use a 20 cm / 8 inch standard round tin. This is what our mothers used, so it is good enough for us.

175 g / 6 oz / 1 ½ sticks unsalted butter
175 g / 6 oz / ¾ cup golden caster (superfine) sugar
3 eggs
150 g / 5 oz / 1 ¼ cups plain (all purpose) flour
30 g / 1 oz / ¼ cup ground almonds
2 teaspoons baking powder
1 teaspoon lemon zest
1-2 tablespoons of milk
200 g / 7 oz / 2 cup glacé cherries

125 g / 4 oz / 1 cup icing (confectioners') sugar
juice of a lemon
30 g / 1 oz flaked almonds
6 glacé cherries, halved

Preheat oven to 180 C / 350 F / Gas 4. Take 1 tablespoon of flour and toss the whole cherries in it to coat. Grease and line a 20 cm / 8 inch cake tin, ideally a spring-form tin.

Cream the butter and sugar till light and fluffy. Add the eggs one at a time, beating between additions. If the mixture looks like it will split, just add a tablespoon of flour.

Sift together the flour and baking powder. Fold into the creamed mixture, stir in the milk to make a thick pourable mixture. Do not over mix. Fold in two thirds of the floured cherries. Pour it into the cake tin. Sprinkle the remaining floured cherries over the top of the mixture.

Bake for 50 minutes to one hour until the cake is cooked and a skewer inserted in the middle comes out clean.

Allow to cool in the tin for 10 minutes then turn out onto a rack to finish cooling.

Toast the slivered almonds until golden. Cool. Make the icing by mixing sifted icing (confectioners') sugar with enough of the lemon juice to make a drizzling consistency. Drizzle over the cake in a random manner (unleash your inner Jackson Pollock). Sprinkle with toasted flaked almonds and halved cherries.

CHERRY SANDWICH CAKE

This is a beautiful cake, with the cherry jam and cream sandwiched between cherry sponges. Ideally the cherries should, of course, be evenly distributed throughout the cake but if disaster strikes and they sink to a sullen layer at the bottom of each sponge you can simply say you are following the view of that renowned gourmand Dick, as expressed in one of Enid Blyton's *Famous Five* books: 'I like this kind of cherry cake,' said Dick, looking at his enormous slice. 'The cherries have all gone to the bottom. They make a very nice last mouthful!' (We have Jane Brocket to thank for reminding us of one of Jane's favourite childhood books.)

225 g / 7 ½ oz / 2 sticks soft butter
225 g / 7 ½ oz / 1 cup caster sugar
4 eggs
225 g / 7 ½ oz / 1 ⁴/₅ cups self-raising flour
2 teaspoons baking powder
200 g / 7 oz glacé cherries
150-170 ml / 5-6 fl oz / ⅔-¾ cup double (heavy) cream, whipped
⅓-½ jar cherry conserve (use conserve rather than jam as it contains more fruit)
caster (superfine) sugar, to decorate

Preheat the oven to 180 C / 350 F / Gas 4. Grease two 20 cm / 8 inch loose-bottomed sandwich tins and line the bases with baking parchment. Sprinkle with flour, tipping away any excess.

Rinse the cherries and cut into quarters. Pat dry on kitchen paper. Put a couple of spoonfuls of the flour into a shallow bowl and add the cherries. Toss until they are well coated; this should stop them sinking to the bottom of the cakes.

Put the butter and sugar into a bowl and cream together. Beat in the eggs, one at a time and then fold in the flour and baking powder. Add the cherries and remaining flour and fold in. Divide the mixture between the tins and level out.

Bake for about 25-30 minutes or until well risen. The top should spring back when lightly pressed and a skewer inserted in the middle should come out clean.

Allow to cool in the tin for 10 minutes, then turn out onto a rack and remove the paper. Once the cakes are cooled, put the bottom half on the plate you want to serve it on; moving finished cakes is always tempting catastrophe. Level the top if necessary and spread conserve and cream evenly over it. Put the other layer on top and dust with caster (superfine) sugar.

PINEAPPLE AND CHERRY UPSIDE-DOWN CAKE

This is a childhood classic and as such should be respected. Don't even think for a second about upgrading this with fresh pineapples or fresh cherries; its full glory is only revealed with tinned (canned) pineapple rings and glacé cherries. You can serve this warm as dessert (perhaps with a little cream or custard) or let it cool and serve as a cake. The method of making caramel was a revelation to us, akin to Ottolenghi's meringues (thank you, Jason Atherton). It makes this notoriously tricky process (admit it, how many times has your caramel crystallized?) a dream. One thing to remember when turning this cake out is that the top is essentially melted sugar, so let it sit for a few minutes and approach with caution; sugar burns are no fun.

Serves 8

For the topping
175 g / 6 oz / ¼ cup caster (superfine) sugar
1 medium tin (can) of pineapple rings (250 g / 8 oz drained weight)
handful of glacé cherries

For the cake
175 g / 6 oz / 1 ½ sticks unsalted butter
175 g / 6 oz / ¾ cup caster (superfine) sugar
4 eggs
1 teaspoon vanilla essence (extract)
175 g / 6 oz / 1 ½ cups plain flour
2 teaspoons baking powder

Preheat the oven to 180 C / 350 F / Gas 4. Grease and line a 24 cm / 9 inch cake tin. Drain the pineapple rings reserving the juice.

Put the first measure of sugar into a cold heavy-bottomed frying (sauté) pan over a low heat and heat gently, stirring to ensure the sugar melts evenly. Watch this like a hawk and when the sugar has completely melted and turned a beautiful golden-brown colour pour into the prepared cake tin to give a thin even layer. Arrange the pineapple rings in an aesthetically pleasing manner over the caramel and place a glacé cherry in the middle of each ring and in any gaps (you can never add too many cherries).

Cream the butter and sugar until light and fluffy. Sift together the flour and baking powder. Beat in the eggs one at a time adding a tablespoon or so of the flour mix after each egg to prevent the mixture curdling. Stir in the rest of the flour to form a smooth batter. Add 1-2 tablespoons of the reserved pineapple juice to form a soft dropping consistency. Spoon over the caramel pineapple and bake on a central rack in the oven for 50 minutes or until a skewer inserted in the centre of the cake comes out clean.

Rest on a rack for 5 minutes then turn out onto a serving plate. Serve warm or cold.

CHERRY AND POPPYSEED FRIANDS

Despite the French-sounding name, friands are most popular in Australia and New Zealand. They are a little light cakey morsel, a cross between a cupcake and a madeleine. Friands can be flavoured with anything from lemon to blueberry and we have developed our own cherry and poppyseed version, the poppyseeds providing a satisfying texture. Traditionally, friands are not iced, but we are not women to let tradition stand between us and a good frosting, so we have topped ours with a fresh cherry buttercream. You can keep them plain (thus kidding yourself they are a diet option) or just make the buttercream to fill and top a Victoria sponge.

Makes 12

150 g / 5 oz / 1 ⅓ sticks butter
175 g / 6 oz / 1 ²/₅ cups icing (confectioners') sugar
45 g / 1 ½ oz / ⅓ cup plain (all purpose) flour

CHERRIES & MULBERRIES

125 g / 4 oz / 1 cup ground almonds
1 tablespoon poppyseeds
4 egg whites
100 g / 3 ½ oz / ¾ cup fresh cherries, pitted and chopped

Icing
60 g / 2 oz / ½ stick butter
150 g / 5 ½ oz / 1 ¼ cup icing (confectioners') sugar
50 g / 1 ¾ oz / ½ cup fresh cherries

Preheat the oven to 200 C / 400 F / gas 6. Line a 12-hole fairy cake or muffin tray with cake cases.

Melt the butter in a saucepan or the microwave and set aside to cool. Sift the flour and icing (confectioners') sugar into a bowl. Stir in the ground almonds and poppyseeds. Stir in the cooled melted butter.

In a separate bowl beat the egg whites to firm peaks. Add a quarter of the egg whites to the dry ingredients and stir in. Stir in the cherry pieces. Fold in the remainder of the egg whites. Do not over mix.

Put into the cake cases and bake for 15-20 minutes until golden and a skewer inserted into the middle of the cake comes out clean. Cool for 10 minutes in the tin and then remove and cool completely on a rack.

Stone and chop the cherries. Cream the butter and half the sugar, beat in the cherries, add the remainder of the icing (confectioners') sugar and beat to a pipeable consistency. There will still be a few small cherry pieces.

You can just pipe or dollop the frosting onto the friands in their cases, but we prefer to take them out first so you can see the little cakes – the cases are really just to form the shape and to save on washing up!

BLACK FOREST GÂTEAU

According to one of our recipe testers Black Forest Gâteau is 'one of man's greatest achievements', up there with the Pyramids and the wheel. It was originally trendy in the 1980s but is now enjoying a much-deserved comeback. There are two versions, one for when you can get fresh cherries and one for the rest of the year, so you can enjoy it at any time. You can use black or morello cherries; morellos have a sharper taste but compliment chocolate very well.

Serves 6-8

For the cake
225 g / 8 oz / 1½ cups self-raising flour
2 teaspoons baking powder
2 tablespoons cocoa
225 g / 8 oz / 2 sticks unsalted butter, soft
225 g / 8 oz / 1 cup caster sugar
4 large eggs

For the decoration
600 g / 1 lb 3 ½ oz / 2 ¾ cups cherries and 60 g / 2 oz / ¼ cup caster sugar OR
200 g / 7 oz cherry conserve (use conserve rather than jam as you get more whole fruits)
4 teaspoons kirsch
350 ml / 12 fl oz / 1 ½ cups double cream

60 g / 2 oz dark chocolate (you only need 20 g / ¾ oz if using conserve)

Preheat the oven to 170 C / 325 F / Gas 3 and grease two 20 cm / 8 inch cake tins with removable bases. Lightly dust the sides with flour and then shake out to remove any excess. Line the bases with baking paper.

Sift the flour, baking powder and cocoa into a large bowl. Add the butter, sugar and eggs. Mix roughly with a fork so the flour doesn't fly everywhere and then mix with an electric hand whisk, moving the whisk so you get as much air as possible into the mixture. You can mix it in a processor but the cake may not rise well, as you won't get as much air into it. Add 1 or 2 tablespoons of warm water so the mixture plops off a spoon.

Divide the mixture between the two tins and bake in the middle of the oven for about 40 minutes until a skewer comes cleanly out of the centre.

Leave to cool for a minute or two, then run a knife round the edge and turn the cakes out onto a wire rack, removing the paper from the base.

Grate 20 g of the chocolate, using a peeler so you get bigger shavings. Set aside. Select about six to eight cherries with stalks to decorate the top of the cake.

Set a large pan of water or the bottom half of a bain-marie on a high heat, bring to the boil and turn off the heat. Immediately place the chocolate, broken into pieces, into the top half of the bain-marie or a heatproof bowl over the water and leave to melt. Holding the cherries by their stalks, coat the fruits in chocolate, swirling them around till they are completely covered. Put them to set on a piece of greaseproof paper. It doesn't matter if the chocolate runs down and forms a pool at the base of each cherry; this will be hidden by the cream on top of the cake.

Pit the rest of the cherries, remove any stalks and put them into a small saucepan with the sugar and kirsch. Simmer until the cherries are soft, stirring gently. Drain the syrup into a jug (this makes a delicious sauce for people who want their cake really gooey) and leave to cool. If you are using conserve simply mix it with the kirsch.

Whip the cream so it forms soft peaks. Level the surface of one cake and spread the fruit and about half the cream onto it. Put the second cake on top and spread the remaining cream on the top of the cake. Embed the chocolate-covered cherries in the cream and sprinkle with the chocolate. Keep the cake in the fridge and then serve with the sauce on the side.

CHERRY SCONES

Scones are an essential part of afternoon tea and these are a delicious variation on traditional fruit scones. Make sure the dried cherries don't have any extra sugar added or your scones will be too sweet. The trick to making really good scones is to be gentle; mix lightly with your fingertips and let the weight of the rolling pin do the flattening; don't push down on the dough.

Makes about 15-18 scones

450 g / 15 oz / 3 3/5 cups self-raising flour
pinch salt
1 tablespoon baking powder
1 tablespoon caster (superfine) sugar
100 g / 3 ½ oz / 7 tablespoons chilled butter, cut into cubes
100 g / 3 ½ oz dried cherries, chopped OR 120 g / 4 oz glacé
cherries, chopped
300 ml / 10 fl oz / 1 ¼ cups milk

Preheat the oven to 220 C / 425 F / Gas 7. Lightly grease a baking sheet. Sift the flour, salt and baking powder into a large bowl and add the sugar and butter. Mix lightly, using your fingertips till the mixture resembles breadcrumbs. This is better done by hand rather than in a mixer as the latter can make the scones stodgy. Add the cherries and mix well.

Make a well in the centre and pour in most of the milk. Using a fork, combine the mixture to form a soft, sticky dough. You may not need all the milk. Mix gently and don't handle the dough more than you need or the scones will lose their light texture.

Turn the dough onto a floured surface and form into a disc. Gently roll out till it is about 2.5 cm / 1 inch thick. Using a round 6 cm or 8 cm / 2 ½ or 3 inch pastry cutter dipped in flour, cut the dough, turning the cutter as you push down. This will give the scones rough sides which will allow them to rise better. Place them on the prepared baking sheet and brush the tops with milk to glaze.

Bake the scones for about 15 minutes. Check them after 12 minutes; they should be well risen and just turning golden brown. Cool on a wire rack.

The scones can be served hot buttered or with cream and jam or curd (see page 118).

MULBERRY AND WHITE CHOCOLATE BISCUITS

One of the most important dates in culinary history was 1977. This was when the recipe for Delia Smith's Chocolate Orange Biscuits appeared in her *Book of Cakes*. Over the years we have adapted it for all manner of fruits and nuts, combining them with dark, milk or white chocolate. A word of warning: dried mulberries are not pretty, particularly white ones. They look unappetizingly like something you might put on a fishing hook. Don't worry though, they turn a golden brown once the biscuits are cooked and give them a lovely chewiness.

Makes 25-30 biscuits

125 g / 4 oz / 1 stick soft butter
175 g / 6 oz / 1 cup caster (superfine) sugar
225 g / 8 oz / 2 cups plain (all purpose) flour
2 teaspoons baking powder
75 g / 3 oz / ½ cup white chocolate, chopped into small chunks
100 g / 3 ½ oz dried mulberries,
1 scant tablespoon orange juice

Heat the oven to 180 C / 350 F / Gas 4.

Beat the butter and sugar together till pale and creamy. Sift the flour and baking powder and mix well. Add the rest of the ingredients and mix together. You should have a stiff, slightly crumbly dough. Don't be tempted to add too much orange juice.

Lightly flour a worktop and roll out the dough. If you want thin biscuits roll them to ¾ cm / ⅓ inch, for chunkier ones roll to 1 ¼ cm / ½ inch. It will be very crumbly but that doesn't matter, just squish it together. The biscuits will hold together once cooked. Cut into 5 cm / 2 inch rounds and place on a greased baking tray (cookie sheet). Allow an inch or so between the biscuits as they spread a lot. Bake on the top shelf for about 10-12 minutes until golden, be careful not to burn them. Leave to cool on the baking tray (cookie sheet) for a couple of minutes to firm up and then transfer to a wire rack to cool fully. In the unlikely event that any are left, these biscuits can be stored in an airtight tin.

Black Forest Brownies

The combination of dried and fresh cherries in these brownies gives a perfect balance of flavour and chewiness. The important thing is not to overcook them or they will turn into a tray of slightly dry cake (you can remedy the matter with icing, but you will have a tray of not brilliant cakes rather than one of deliciously gooey brownies). Cook until just set, or when a knife or skewer inserted in the middle comes out with just a few moist crumbs.

Makes 16

155 g / 5 oz / 1 ¼ cups plain (all-purpose) flour
¼ tsp salt
110 g / 4 oz good quality plain (bittersweet) chocolate
110 g / 4 oz / 1 stick unsalted butter
150 g / 5 oz / ⅔ cup dark soft brown sugar
150 g / 5 oz / ⅔ cup caster (superfine) sugar

2 eggs

125 g / 4 oz fresh cherries, pitted, destalked and chopped roughly into quarters

50 g / 1 ¾ oz dried cherries, chopped if they are large

Preheat the oven to 180 C / 350 F / Gas 4. Line a 23 cm / 9 inch square baking tin (cake pan) with baking parchment.

Sift the flour and salt into a large bowl.

Melt the chocolate and butter in a bain-marie or heatproof bowl set over just boiled water. Add the sugars and leave for 5 minutes to dissolve slightly, then tip into a large bowl and stir to mix well.

Beat in the eggs one by one to make a glossy mixture. Add the fresh and dried cherries and stir through. Gently fold in the flour. You want an even brown coloured mix (not streaky) but don't over mix.

Pour the mixture into the prepared baking tin (cake pan) to form an even layer. Bake for 30-45 minutes or until just set in the middle. The cooking time will depend on the juiciness of your cherries; the more moist the brownie mixture is, the longer it will take to cook. Check at about 30 minutes and if it is not ready turn the oven down to 170 C / 325 F / Gas 3 and cook for a little longer. A knife inserted in the centre should come out with just a few moist crumbs and if you listen to the brownies they should be quiet rather than making a bubbling sound (yes, we know this seems daft but it works). Cool completely in the pan before cutting into squares.

Mount Fuji Cakes

These cakes were inspired by the view of Mount Fuji with the cherry trees in bloom around its base. Inside each cake is a hidden core of cherry 'lava'. To create the mountain effect, you need conical or pyramid-shaped silicone moulds, which can be bought fairly easily at specialist cook shops or online. The cakes taste just as good baked as muffins but aren't nearly as much fun.

Makes 6 cakes

Cake
110 g / 4 oz / 1 stick butter
125 g / 4 oz / ½ cup caster (superfine) sugar
2 eggs
125 g / 4 oz / 1 cup self-raising flour, sifted
1 tablespoon cherry concentrate

Filling
1 tablespoon cherry conserve or jam

Icing
280 g / 9 oz / 2 ¼ cups icing (confectioners') sugar
1 tablespoon cherry concentrate
small lump of fondant icing (for the 'snow' on each cake)

Preheat the oven to 180 C / 350 F / Gas 4. Grease the pyramids with a thin layer of oil.

Put the butter and sugar into a bowl and cream together. Beat in the eggs, one at a time, adding a spoonful of flour after each egg. Then add the cherry concentrate and mix well. Gently fold in the flour, being careful not to squash the air out of the mixture.

Divide the mixture between the moulds and level out. If you are making 'volcanoes' rather than muffins, you will find you have made slightly more mixture than you need as the cakes will need a flat surface to stand on. Either make a small seventh or lick the bowl clean. Bake for about 20 minutes until a skewer comes out clean and the tops spring back when lightly pressed.

Leave to cool for a few moments, level the bases with a sharp knife and then turn out onto a wire rack. Allow the cakes to cool completely.

Using an apple corer, remove a 'core' from the base of each cake. Be careful not to burst though the top of the cake. Using a teaspoon, drop a little conserve into each hole. Cut the top off the plug of cake to allow space for the jam and replace it to seal the jam inside.

Don't be tempted to insert too much jam; you want to create a little surprise, not a jammy mess.

Sift the icing (confectioners') sugar into a bowl, add the cherry conserve and mix well. Add a little more water if necessary; you want a fairly thick but just spreadable mixture. Spread evenly over the cakes. Leave to set.

Roll the fondant so it is as thin as it will get without falling apart. Using a pointed knife, cut six rough circles which will form the snow on the top of the mountains. Place a circle of fondant on the top of each cake and gently press into shape.

School Birthday Cake

Jane went to a traditional Enid Blyton boarding school and, along with midnight feasts and food parcels from home, birthday teas were one of the culinary highlights of the year. The village bakery had a selection of cakes you could choose from. All were good but the Chocolate Biscuit Cake stood out as being by far and away the best. Luckily, some years ago the school produced a recipe book and Rachel Good (who was at the school years later) had provided a recipe for the cake. Our version is slightly different (Jane is convinced it is nearer to the original) and the cherries are not authentic but, like many things, they are an added improvement.

This cake is rich and should serve about twelve. However, if you are feeding hungry schoolgirls, gannet-like estate agents or Jane, reduce that number to nearer eight.

Cake
250 g / 8 oz milk chocolate
200 g / 7 oz / 1 ¾ sticks butter
2 tablespoons milk
400 g / 14 oz digestive biscuits, crushed finely
150 g / 5 oz fresh cherries or 100 g / 3 ½ oz dried cherries

Icing
100 g / 3 ½ oz good quality milk chocolate
OR
80 g / 2 ½ oz good quality milk chocolate
100 g / 3 ½ oz / ¾ stick butter, softened
100 g / 3 ½ oz / ⁴/₅ cup icing (confectioners') sugar

Decoration
Toffee cherries (page 146) OR a handful of cherries with stalks

Lightly grease a 20 cm / 8 inch cake tin and line the base with baking paper.

It is easier if you make the cake in two layers, otherwise there are a lot of biscuit crumbs to mix. Put half the chocolate, half the butter and 1 tablespoon of milk in a bowl over a saucepan of simmering water. Stir occasionally until melted and combined.

Put half the crushed digestive biscuits into a large bowl, add the melted chocolate mixture and mix well so all the biscuit pieces are coated in chocolate.

Spoon the biscuit mixture into the tin and press down well. If using fresh cherries, pit and cut in half. If your dried cherries are large, cut them in half too. Spread the cherries evenly over the cake. Mix the remaining chocolate, butter, milk and biscuits as above and spread over the top. Press the mixture down firmly, ensuring it gets right to the edge of the tin. Put in the fridge to cool and set.

Remove the cake from the tin. If you are topping the cake with chocolate, melt the milk chocolate in a bowl over hot water. Spread evenly over the top of the cake.

If you are using icing, melt the milk chocolate in a bowl over hot water. Sieve the icing sugar if necessary (i.e. only if there are large lumps, we don't usually bother) into a large bowl and add the butter. Mix gently at first so the icing sugar doesn't fly everywhere, and then beat until it is soft and creamy. Mix in the melted chocolate. Put the icing in the fridge for about 20 minutes to firm up a bit and spread over the top and sides.

Put the remaining cherries on top or decorate the cake as appropriate for the occasion; it seems a shame to only use it for birthday cakes, unless you have a lot of friends with birthdays spread conveniently throughout the year.

Put the cake in the fridge for at least half an hour to set, if you can leave it overnight it will be better.

Tottenham Cake

This popular traybake (sheet cake) was reputedly created by a Quaker baker (we love the alliteration) who made it to celebrate the 1901 victory of Tottenham Hotspur football team in the 1901 FA Cup Final. There was a Friends Meeting House in Tottenham Fields and this reputedly provided the mulberries used in the icing. Henry Chalker (the Quaker baker) sold Tottenham Cake ever after at a penny a piece or a halfpenny for misshapes. Whether this is true or not (as with all good tales there is some doubt) it makes a charming story. Today it is, far more prosaically, sold by Greggs. We usually prefer butter in baking but the original recipe had margarine – take your pick.

Serves 8-10

175 g / 6 oz / ¾ cup margarine or butter
175 g / 6 oz / 1 cup caster (superfine) sugar
3 eggs
250 g / 8 oz / 2 cups self-raising flour
1 teaspoon vanilla essence
a little grated nutmeg
1-2 tablespoons milk if required

Icing
125 g / 4 oz / 1 cup icing (confectioners') sugar
mulberry juice
squeeze of lemon juice (optional)

Grease and line a 25 cm / 10 inch square cake tin. Preheat the oven to 150 C / 300 F / Gas 2.

Cream the margarine or butter and sugar until light and fluffy. Beat in the eggs adding a tablespoon of the flour after each egg so the mixture doesn't split. Add the vanilla essence (extract) and nutmeg. Fold in the remaining flour. If required stir in up to two tablespoons of milk to make a soft dropping consistency.

Pour into the tray and bake for around 50 minutes or until a skewer inserted in the centre of the cake comes out clean. Turn out onto a rack and allow to cool.

Sieve the icing (confectioners') sugar into a bowl and add the mulberry juice gradually to get a smooth spreadable consistency. Add a squirt of lemon juice if the icing seems too sweet. Spread the icing over the top of the cake and leave to set. Cut into squares to serve.

GLOSSARY

ACID: soil with a pH of less than 7.

ALKALINE: soil with a pH of more than 7.

ANTHER: the male part of the flower. Pollen must be transferred from here to the (female) stigma for fruit to develop.

BARE-ROOTED: plants sold during their dormant season without soil around their roots.

CULTIVAR: a variety within a species, cultivated by man. These are frequently (and wrongly) called varieties.

ESPALIER: a tree trained against a flat support: either a fence, wall, or posts and wires. The central stem rises vertically, the side shoots are trained out horizontally on either side.

FAMILY: the category of plant classification which includes a group of related genera. It is botanically important but is not usually given on horticultural labels.

FAN: the stems of the plant are spread out against a support, typically a fence or wall, and trained into a fan shape by pruning and tying-in.

FEATHERED MAIDEN: a young tree with side shoots (feathers), usually two years old.

FLOWERS, SINGLE: one layer of petals.

FLOWERS, DOUBLE: usually around 30 individual, tightly-packed petals creating rounded flowers.

FLOWERS, SEMI-DOUBLE: two or more layers of petals.

GENUS (plural genera): the category of plant classification between family and species. It is based on the plant's botanical characteristics and is indicated by its first Latin name.

GRAFT UNION: the point on the trunk where the scion joins the rootstock.

HANAMI: the traditional Japanese custom of viewing spring blossom, usually cherries. The festivals involve picnics beneath the trees, drinking tea or sake, and pinning slips of paper with poems (*tanzaku*) onto the trees.

HYBRID: the offspring of plants of two different species or genera.

LATERAL: side-shoot growing off the main stem.

LEADER: the main stem of the plant.

MAIDEN WHIP: a one-year-old tree with no side shoots

ORGANIC MATTER: natural material that can be used as a soil improver or mulch, such as well-rotted farmyard manure, garden compost or composted straw.

pH: this refers to the acidity or alkalinity of the soil. pH7 is neutral, above is alkaline, below is acid.

PHENOLIC ANTIOXIDANTS: a class of antioxidant found in some plants and fruit which offers resistance to some illnesses.

POLLINATION: the transfer of pollen from the anther to the stamen. It is necessary for the flowers to develop into fruits. (see self-fertile and self-infertile)

PROPAGATING: making new plants from seeds, cuttings, layering or division.

ROOTSTOCK: the lower part of a grafted tree below the graft. This will usually determine the size of the tree.

SAKURA: the blossom of Japanese ornamental cherry trees

SCION: the upper part of a grafted tree above the graft. It will determine the type of fruit.

SELF-FERTILE: a plant whose flowers can self-pollinate, i.e. a flower which can be pollinated by its own pollen or by that from another flower on the same plant.

SELF-STERILE or SELF-INFERTILE: a plant whose flowers cannot pollinate themselves. To produce fruit the tree needs to be near a compatible cultivar.

SERICULTURE: the cultivation of silkworms for silk.

SORBITOL: a sweet tasting crystalline compound found in some fruit.

SPECIES (sp. plural spp.): the category of classification below genus consisting of botanically closely related plants. The species is indicated by the plant's second Latin name.

STIGMA: the female part of the flower. Pollen must be transferred here from the (male) anther for fruit to develop.

TANZAKU: slips of paper with poems or wishes written on them which are attached to trees at *hanami*. The poems can be copied from a master or composed on the spot.

'THREE Ds': dead, diseased and damaged branches

UNIVERSAL POLLINATOR: a cherry cultivar which will pollinate any other cultivar flowering at the same time.

USDA ZONES: United States Department of Agriculture zones which are based on the average annual minimum temperatures and indicate in which areas a plant will thrive.

VERNALIZATION: a period of low temperature below 0° C / 32° F which is needed to break dormancy and induce flowering in some plants, particularly cherry and many other fruit trees.

WINTER CHILLING: see vernalization.

BIBLIOGRAPHY

The books are roughly divided by subject, but many of the gardening books have interesting historical information and many of the historical books contain useful horticultural hints. And all of them often have delicious recipes scattered about.

THE STORIES OF CHERRIES AND MULBERRIES

Bates, H. E. *The Wild Cherry Tree*, Michael Joseph, 1968

The Bible: King James Version with The Apocrypha, Penguin Classics, 2006

Campbell-Culver, Maggie. *A Passion for Trees: The Legacy of John Evelyn*, Eden Project Books, 2006

Capote, Truman. *In Cold Blood: A True Account of a Multiple Murder and its Consequences*, Penguin Classics, 2000

Carey, Frances. *The Tree: Meaning and Myth*, British Museum Press, 2012

Chekhov, Anton. *The Cherry Orchard*, translated by Constance Garnett, Chatto & Windus, 1923

Clifford, Sue and King, Angela (for Common Ground). *England in Particular*, Hodder & Stoughton, 2006

Davidson, Alan. *The Oxford Companion to Food*, edited by Tom Jaine, Oxford University Press, 2014

Davidson, Alan and Knox, Charlotte. *Fruit: A Connoisseur's Guide and Cookbook*, Mitchell Beazley, 1991

Greenoak, Francesca. *Forgotten Fruit*, Andre Deutsch, 1983

Grigson, Geoffrey. T*he Englishman's Flora*, Phoenix House, 1958

Hatfield, Gabrielle. *Hatfield's Herbal*, Allen Lane, 2007

Herodotus. *The Histories,* translated by George Rawlinson, Everyman's Library, 1997

Herrick, Robert. *The Poetical Works*, Oxford University Press, 1921

Housman, A. E. *A Shropshire Lad*, Hesperus Press, 2008

Johnson, Hugh. *Trees*, Mitchell Beazley, 2010

Lawrence, D. H. *Selected Poems*, Penguin Classics, 2008

Lawrence, D. H. *Sons and Lovers*, Penguin Classics, 2006

Mabey, Richard. *Flora Britannica*, Sinclair-Stevenson, 1996

McClellan, Ann. *The Cherry Blossom Festival*, Bunker Hill Publication, 2005

Mayhew, Henry. *London Labour and the London Poor*, Wordsworth Editions, 2008

Mason, Laura. *The Taste of Britain*, HarperPress, 2006

Palter, Robert. *The Duchess of Malfi's Apricots and Other Literary Fruits*, University of South Carolina Press, 2002

Parkinson, Anna. *Nature's Alchemist: John Parkinson, Herbalist to Charles I*, Frances Lincoln Ltd, 2007

Penguin Book of English Verse, edited by Paul Keegan, Penguin Classics, 2001

Pepys, Samuel. *The Diary of Samuel Pepys*, edited by Robert Latham and William Matthews, G. Bell and Sons / Bell and Hyman, 11 volumes, 1970-1983

Potter, Jennifer. *Strange Blooms: the Curious Lives and Adventures of the John Tradescants*, Atlantic Books, 2006

Roach, F. A. *The Cultivated Fruits of Britain*, Blackwell, 1985

Roberts, Jonathan. *Cabbages and Kings*, HarperCollins, 2001

Shikibu, Murasaki. *The Tale of Genji*, translated by Edward Seidensticker, Everyman's Library, 1992

Stafford, Fiona. *The Long, Long Life of Trees*, Yale University Press, 2016

Stuart, David C. *The Kitchen Garden: A Historical Guide to Traditional Crops*, Robert Hale, 1984

Szabó, Magda. *The Door*, translated by Len Rix, Harvill Secker, 2005

Tolstoy, Leo, *The Kreutzer Sonata and Other Stories*, translated by Louise and Aylmer Maude and J. D. Duff, Oxford University Press, 1998

Uglow, Jenny. *A Little History of British Gardening*, Chatto & Windus, 2004

Ulak, James T. and Kaplan, Howard. *Cherry Blossoms*, Skira Rizzoli Publications, 2015

CHERRIES AND MULBERRIES
FOR HEALTH

Blythman, Joanna. *What to Eat: Food that's Good for Your Health, Pocket and Plate*, Fourth Estate, 2013

McGee, Harold. *On Food and Cooking*, Hodder & Stoughton, 2004

Neal's Yard Remedies: Healing Foods, edited by Susannah Steel, Dorling Kindersley, 2013

Pollan, Michael. *In Defence of Food: The Myth of Nutrition and the Pleasure of Eating*, Penguin Books, 2009

Wills, Judith. *The Food Bible*, Quadrille, 2007

CHERRIES AND MULBERRIES
IN THE GARDEN

Don, Monty. *The Ivington Diaries*, Bloomsbury Publishing, 2009

Flowerdew, Bob. *Complete Fruit Book*, Kyle Cathie Limited, 1995

Hill, Lewis and Perry, Leonard. *The Fruit Gardener's Bible*, Storey Publishing, 2011

Sieur Le Gendre. *The Manner of Ordering Fruit Trees*, translated by John Evelyn, Early English Books Online Editions, 2017

Lyle, Susanna. *Ultimate Fruit and Nuts*, Frances Lincoln, 2006

McMorland Hunter, Jane. *The Tiny Garden*, Frances Lincoln, 2006

McMorland Hunter, Jane and Kelly, Chris. *For the Love of an Orchard*, Pavilion, 2010

McMorland Hunter, Jane and Kelly, Chris. *Teach Yourself Basic Gardening*, Hodder Educational, 2010

More, David and White, John. *Cassell's Trees of Britain and Northern Europe*, Cassell, 2003

Pearson, Dan. *Natural Selection: A Year in the Garden*, Guardian Books and Faber & Faber, 2017

Pike, Ben. *The Fruit Tree Handbook*, Green Books, 2011

Reich, Lee. *Landscaping with Fruit*, Storey Publishing, 2009

Reich, Lee. *Uncommon Fruits Worthy of Attention*, Addison-Wesley Publishing Company, 1991

Royal Horticultural Society A-Z Encyclopedia of Garden Plants, editor-in-chief Christopher Brickell, Dorling Kindersley, 2008

RHS Plant Finder 2017, Royal Horticultural Society, 2017

Swift, Katherine. *The Morville Year*, Bloomsbury Publishing, 2011

Books on fruit by the following are inspiring and informative: Richard Bird, Alan Buckingham, Mark Diacono, Dr D.G. Hessayon, Carol Klein and Alan Titchmarsh.

HISTORICAL COOKERY, GARDENING BOOKS AND HERBALS

Acton, Eliza. *Modern Cookery for Private Families*, Southover Press, 2011

Beeton's Book of Household Management, edited by Mrs Isabella Beeton, a facsimile of the first edition of 1861, Southover Press, 1996

Bunyard, Edward. *The Anatomy of Dessert*, Modern Library Series, Random House USA, 2006

Culpeper, Nicholas. *The Complete Herbal*, Harvey Sales, 1981

Digby, Sir Kenelm. *The Closet of Sir Kenelm Digby Opened*, edited by Jane Stevenson and Peter Davidson, Prospect Books, 1997

Evelyn, John. *The Diary of John Evelyn*, edited by E. S. de Beer, selected and introduced by Roy Strong, Everyman's Library, 2006

Gerard, John. *Leaves from Gerard's Herball*, arranged by Marcus Woodward, John Lane / Bodley Head, 1943

Glasse, Hannah. *First Catch Your Hare: The Art of Modern Cookery Made Plain and Easy*, a facsimile of the first edition, 1747, Prospect Books, 1995

Lawson, William. *A New Orchard and Garden* with *The Country Housewife's Garden,* Prospect Books, 2003

MacGregor, Jessie. *Gardens of Celebrities and Celebrated Gardens in and Around London*, Hutchinson, 1918

Nott, John. *The Cooks and Confectioners Dictionary: Or, the Accomplish'd Housewives Companion*, introduction and glossary by Elizabeth David, Lawrence Rivington, 1980

Pliny the Elder. *Natural History*, translated by John F. Healey, Penguin Classics, 1991

CHERRIES AND MULBERRIES IN THE KITCHEN

Alexander, Stephanie. *The Cook's Companion*, Penguin, 2007

Atherton, Jason. *Maze*, Quadrille, 2007

BBC Good Food Magazine, Immediate Media

Books for Cooks Volumes 1-10, Pryor Publications, 2001 onwards

Benenden School Cookbook, Benenden School Seniors' Association, 2004

Blyton, Enid. *Five go to Mystery Moor*, Hodder & Stoughton, 1954

Brocket, Jane. *Cherry Cake and Ginger Beer*, Hodder & Stoughton, 2008

Bunyard, Edward. *The Anatomy of Dessert*, Modern Library, 2006

Fearnley-Whittingstall, Hugh. *River Cottage Fruit Every Day*, Bloomsbury, 2013

Grigson, Jane. *Jane Grigson's Fruit Book*, Penguin Books, 2000

Palmer, John (ed.). *The Cook's Scrapbook*, Reader's Digest, 1995

Prince, Thane. *Perfect Preserves*, Hodder & Stoughton, 2014

Raven, Sarah. *Sarah Raven's Garden Cookbook*, Bloomsbury, 2007

Slater, Nigel. *Tender, Volume II*, Fourth Estate, 2010

Smith, Delia. *Book of Cakes*, Book Club Associates, 1977

Waters, Alice. *Chez Panisse Fruit*, HarperCollins, 2002

WEBSITES

www.brogdalecollections.org

www.moruslondinium.org

www.spitalfieldslife.com

www.rentacherrytree.co.uk If you don't have room for a cherry tree you can rent your own at Cook's Yard Farm, New Road, Northiam, East Sussex. You can visit the trees in spring to see the blossom and you then receive emails telling you when the fruit is ready to pick.

ACKNOWLEDGEMENTS

We would both like to thank the following:
Everyone at Hatchards and The National Archives for their support of our books.
The National Archives for permission to reproduce the image on page 34 of the Buckingham House Gardens 1760 from their collection.
Catheryn Kilgarriff at Prospect Books who produces such lovely books.
Teresa Chris, our agent, for her continued support.

Jane:
To Ian Prince for finding poems and huge thanks to Mat Goss who proved, beyond doubt, that estate agents have discerning palates. And Matilda, who proved that cats do too.

Sally
To my mother who taught me to love and to cook cake, and in doing so made my life better, to Paul, the world's best greengrocer, and Chris and the team at Millers Butchers who constantly confirm that local shops are always the best, and to Philip Garrett of Leeston whose trees produce the biggest and best mulberries we have ever seen.

Finally, we would like to thank all our friends and family who obligingly adapted to eating cherries and mulberries with almost everything.

INDEX

All recipes are listed alphabetically under RECIPES.